Kindergarten

Credits
Content Editor: Jennifer B. Stith
Copy Editor: Julie B. Killian

Visit *carsondellosa.com* for correlations to Common Core, state, national, and Canadian provincial standards.

Carson-Dellosa Publishing LLC
PO Box 35665
Greensboro, NC 27425 USA
carsondellosa.com

ISBN 978-1-4838-3843-4
01-002187784

Table of Contents

What Is Math Workshop?.............................3

The Elements of Math Workshop.................4

What Does Math Workshop Look Like?.........6

Managing Math Workshop 7

Planning and Preparation 9

Student Expectations.................................11

Ensuring Accountability 13

Counting and Cardinality

Counting...15

Counting by Tens.......................................21

Counting On...27

Reading and Writing Numbers to 20..........33

Connecting Counting to Quantity..............39

Counting Sets 45

Comparing Sets 51

Comparing Numbers..................................57

Operations and Algebraic Thinking

Understanding Addition.............................63

Understanding Subtraction 69

Addition Word Problems 75

Subtraction Word Problems........................81

Decomposing Numbers 87

Making 10..93

Patterning..99

Number and Operations in Base Ten

Tens and Ones...105

Decomposing Numbers 11–19...................111

Measurement and Data

Measurable Attributes................................117

Comparing Objects 123

Classifying and Sorting Objects................129

Graphing Data...135

Calendar Concepts....................................141

Geometry

Relative Positions.......................................147

Shapes...153

Solid Shapes 159

Flat vs. Solid Shapes..................................165

Shape Attributes..171

Composing Shapes.....................................177

Reproducibles

Number of the Day.....................................183

Bump!...184

Four-in-a-Row...185

Path Game 186

Roll and Solve...187

Flip! 188

Shut the Box 189

Answer Key 190

What Is Math Workshop?

One of the most challenging aspects of teaching mathematics is differentiating instruction to meet the needs of all of the learners in your classroom. As a classroom teacher, you are responsible for teaching the standards that must be met by the end of the year. But, the reality inside the classroom is that one size does not fit all. For some students, the material is too difficult. For others, it is too easy.

With both reading and writing, many teachers have found the workshop model to be an excellent way to teach students at various levels. It allows for whole-group and small-group instruction, and individual practice so teachers can monitor students' progress and vary instruction according to need. The same workshop approach can be used for successful math instruction. This model encourages students to go beyond passive learning and become mathematicians who can think critically.

Like reading and writing workshops, math workshop is a structure, not a curriculum. It can be used with existing curriculums and materials and should be adapted to best fit the needs of the teacher and students. Math workshop will look different from classroom to classroom but usually includes the same building blocks: a warm-up, a whole-class mini-lesson, leveled small-group instruction, and individual practice. For a more in-depth look at the elements of math workshop, refer to pages 4 and 5.

Using a math workshop model allows teachers to:
- meet the needs of learners at all levels
- encourage deeper learning than in traditional lessons
- spiral concepts throughout the year
- work with any curriculum
- group students flexibly so they can move according to their changing needs
- offer repeated opportunities for practice
- keep students consistently engaged in learning

Starting math workshop in your classroom can seem overwhelming if you've never done it before. Use the guides on pages 4 through 14 to help you decide how math workshop will work in your classroom, plan your lessons, and manage the day-to-day details. Then, get started with over 25 preplanned lessons and activities. Use the blank reproducible activities starting on page 183 to create your own practice and review activities to be used throughout the year.

The Elements of Math Workshop

The major parts of math workshop are a warm-up, a mini-lesson, rotations (which include guided math groups, independent practice, and conferencing), and closure. You do not have to follow this format exactly. Instead, mix, match, and tweak things to make math workshop work for your classroom. See page 6 for more information on how math workshop can be changed to better fit your needs. Once you understand the basics, you can use the information below to plan your own math workshop lessons. Refer to pages 9 and 10 for more information on planning math workshop lessons.

1 Warm-Up
about 5 minutes

The warm-up is used to get students thinking mathematically and prepare them for the mini-lesson. It can be the same every day, or changed to relate to the lesson focus. You may choose to discuss only a portion of the assignment, such as a few sections of the calendar bulletin board or a single review problem.

Options*:
- number talks or number study
- problem of the day
- calendar time
- quick games (for example, Buzz or Around the World)
- discussion of an incorrectly solved problem
- number of the day (use the template on page 183)
- fact fluency practice
- daily review problems

2 Mini-Lesson
10–15 minutes

The mini-lesson is a teacher-led, whole-group activity. This is when new vocabulary and foundational information should be introduced and modeled. Teachers should model math thinking as they work through example problems. Often, students work with a practice problem to clear up any misconceptions.

Options*:
- present a textbook lesson
- show an introduction video
- solve a problem and think aloud
- demonstrate a new strategy
- direct a hands-on activity
- create an anchor chart
- share a math read-aloud
- review the previous day's lesson

*Please note that the options provided are a starting point and there are many more options you can explore for each section.

3 Rotations 10–20 minutes each

Students rotate through guided math with the teacher, independent practice, and workstations. This is also the time when teachers may choose to skip small group instruction in favor of one-on-one conferencing with students.

Guided Math

During this time, you work with small (eight or fewer students), flexible, leveled groups of students to extend and enhance the mini-lesson. Students use manipulatives to better understand the reasoning, procedures, strategies, etc., of the topic. Focus on using math talk and math tools to make sure students really understand the topic. Begin with the lowest group so they do not work on independent practice until after small-group instruction. Like the mini-lesson, these lessons can follow the warm-up/explanation/guided practice/independent practice/assessment model, although they don't have to.

Independent Stations

This segment is also known as centers, rotations, workstations, etc. Activities can be individual, partner, or small group and often include both practice of the current skill or topic and review of past skills. Activities should be introduced ahead of time so students can work independently and should be at a level that won't produce frustration. Students can follow a strict rotation or may be given daily choices as long as they complete certain set activities each week.

Options*:
- math games and activities
- fact fluency practice
- Solve the Room activities
- technology centers (including online games and district-mandated math programs)
- practice sheets (*Note:* The practice sheets included in the lessons are all different, so students can progress through them as they gain understanding of the skill.)
- journaling and/or interactive notebooks

Conferencing

Instead of leading guided math groups, you may choose to periodically observe students during independent stations or pull students for one-on-one conferencing. This allows for formative assessment and more targeted instruction for students who need more help with a skill. This is also an ideal time to do state- or district-mandated quarterly testing.

4 Closure/ Reflection 3–5 minutes

The closure is a short, targeted way to wrap up the learning students did during math workshop. It is the perfect time to review the math objective or essential question and answer any questions students may still have.

Options*:
- exit tickets
- allow a few students to explain an "ah-ha!" moment they had
- think/pair/share problem-solving
- math talk prompts
- quick journaling
- students can share what they learned in their own words
- Q and A time

*Please note that the options provided are a starting point and there are many more options you can explore for each section.

What Does Math Workshop Look Like?

Due to the nature of the workshop model, math workshop will look different in different classrooms. You can change it however you need so that it works best for your classroom. See below for ideas and examples of how you can reshape math workshop for your needs.

Timing and Structure

- You can conduct math workshop daily, a few times a week, or monthly.
- Or, you can use one or two days to teach longer whole-class lessons and use the remaining days for rotations.
- Meet with each leveled group daily, or only once or twice a week, depending on how long your math block is.
- Have students visit every station daily or visit each station once each week.

Content

- Use your textbook, a prescribed curriculum, or make your own lessons.
- You can have students use math notebooks for recording work and/or journaling.
- Use the same handful of simple games so you don't have to reinvent the wheel (for example, sorting activities, puzzles, concentration, etc.).
- The lessons provided in this book are interchangeable. If you don't like one or more of the suggestions, replace it with your own.

Assessment

- Build in formal assessment as a longer closure, as a station to visit, or take a day off to administer a test.
- You may choose to have students record the results from each activity or use a checklist during rotations.
- See page 13 for more information on accountability during math workshop.

Grouping

- Groups do not have to be the same size.
- You can have more than one group at the same level to ensure small groups.
- To group students, you can use formative assessment, pretests, or group them on the fly after observations made during the previous day or the mini-lesson.
- You can choose to move students between leveled groups as needed (which could even mean daily) or after more formal assessments.

Choice

- You can require students to visit rotations in a certain order and/or on specific days.
- Or, you can allow students to choose which centers to complete each day.
- You may choose to make students responsible for completing all of the rotations by the end of the week, or you can make some rotations mandatory each day (such as independent practice, fact fluency, and technology centers).
- Students can complete rotations at their desks so you can keep an eye on them, or you can allow them to work in various spots around the room.

Managing Math Workshop

Math workshop can be daunting to newcomers because of all of the elements that need preparation and upkeep. However, the tips and suggestions below for managing the various parts of math workshop will help you get started on the right foot and maintain it throughout the year.

Starting and Maintaining Math Workshop

- Set student expectations before beginning. See page 11 for more information.
- Don't underestimate the power of positive reinforcement.
- Stop and practice the routines and procedures as needed throughout the year if students aren't following expectations.
- Start slow! Begin with only one game or activity during rotations.
- Practice any new games or activities with the whole group first.
- Keep it simple. To begin with, use familiar activities such as concentration, war, or dominoes.
- As you introduce new activities through the year, use the same formats so you don't have to teach a new set of rules each time.
- If possible, use assistants or parent volunteers to monitor students during the first few weeks.
- During weeks with field trips, assemblies, etc., try to move math workshop to a different time. Or, use the entire week to review old concepts and meet with groups that need more help with old concepts instead of introducing a new topic.

Organizing Materials

- Keep all of the necessary supplies in the area where you meet for guided math. That way, students don't waste time looking for materials such as pencils, paper, and manipulatives.
- Use bins or baskets to organize activities, games, and small group supplies for guided math, so everything needed to complete the activity is in one easy-to-grab place.
- Make all math manipulatives visible and accessible so students can use whatever tools they need whenever they need to.
- Make several copies of each activity so multiple pairs or groups of students can work on the same one.
- Designate a student or students each week to be the Materials Master. Their job is to make sure all materials are cleaned up and organized each day.

Managing Math Workshop, cont.

Classroom Management

Managing Rotations

- Use a bulletin board, pocket chart, or interactive whiteboard for a visual reminder of the rotations order. Refer to the example below.
- Use self-stick notes with student names to make reorganizing leveled groups quick and easy.
- Use visual cues and directions on games so students can work independently.
- When students are absent, you can catch them up during conferencing/one-on-one time or temporarily move them to a lower group.

Student Behavior

- For early finishers: have review, extension, or older activities available; make a packet with word problems or challenges to complete; or create a chart listing things they can move on to.
- Foster independence with an "ask three before me" policy.
- Have students use a special hand signal so they can ask to use the bathroom without interrupting guided math.
- For students who have trouble working independently, remove them from rotations and have them sit at a desk near the guided math group until they are ready to rejoin rotations. It may be helpful to have those students start back slowly, with only one independent activity reintroduced at a time.

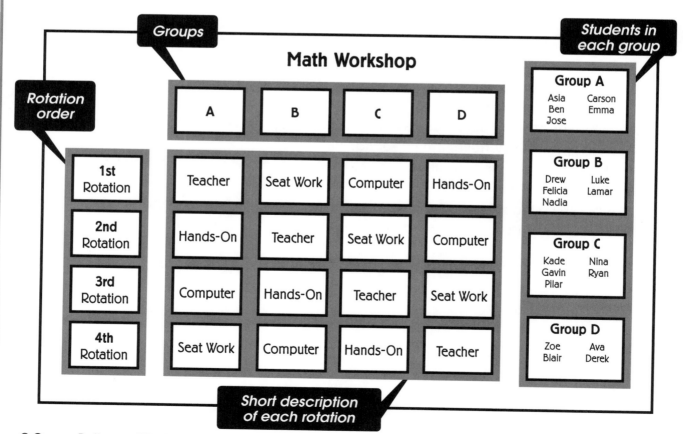

Groups

Students in each group

Rotation order

Math Workshop

	A	B	C	D
1st Rotation	Teacher	Seat Work	Computer	Hands-On
2nd Rotation	Hands-On	Teacher	Seat Work	Computer
3rd Rotation	Computer	Hands-On	Teacher	Seat Work
4th Rotation	Seat Work	Computer	Hands-On	Teacher

Group A
Asia   Carson
Ben   Emma
Jose

Group B
Drew   Luke
Felicia Lamar
Nadia

Group C
Kade   Nina
Gavin   Ryan
Pilar

Group D
Zoe   Ava
Blair   Derek

Short description of each rotation

Planning and Preparation

As with anything, math workshop will be less stressful and have a better chance of success if you plan in advance. Use your district's scope and sequence, textbook curriculum, or similar to plan roughly when and how long to teach each topic. Then, plan the specifics for only a week or two at a time to allow room for remediation or moving on early, depending on what students need. Use the reproducible below to create a high-level plan for a week. Use page 10 to plan more specifically for the guided math groups for that week.

Math Workshop

Week of _____

Objective:	Essential Question:

Mini-Lesson		Rotations
Monday		
Tuesday		
Wednesday		
Thursday		
Friday		

Guided Math

Week of _____

Group 1 Level:	Group 2 Level:
Students:	Students:
Group 3 Level:	**Group 4** Level:
Students:	Students:

	Group 1	Group 2	Group 3	Group 4
Monday				
Tuesday				
Wednesday				
Thursday				
Friday				

Student Expectations

Math workshop will not be perfect from the start. It may be a bit chaotic and students may try to play instead of work. But, by setting student expectations early, and with plenty of practice and modeling, math workshop can run smoothly.

Questions to Consider

How should materials be handled? Will there be dedicated students in charge of the materials? Where will they be stored? When can students access them? How and when should cleanup happen? Should there be a one-minute cleanup warning before switching rotations or is cleaning up part of the transition time? Who is responsible for cleaning up common areas?

How and when can students work with others? What activities should be done alone, with a partner, or as group work? Who and when can students ask for help?

What does staying on task mean in math workshop? What level should the volume be? Where should students be working? How should students be accountable for the work they've done? What should the conversations sound like?

What happens if students make mistakes or struggle? Who can they ask for help? What materials and strategies are available if a problem is too hard? Can they skip difficult problems or save them for conferencing?

When is the teacher available? Can students interrupt guided math groups? How can they signal they need to go to the bathroom? What is an appropriate reason to interrupt the teacher? Who else can help students and answer questions?

Setting Expectations

One of the first things you should do when beginning math workshop is to clearly outline the expectations. While you don't have to do this in tandem with making an anchor chart, the visual reminder can be helpful for retaining the expectations as well as serving as a visual reminder throughout the year.

- It can be helpful to frame the expectations simply: What should math workshop look like? What should it sound like? What is the student responsible for? What is the teacher responsible for? Refer to the Questions to Consider in the section above for more specific things to discuss.
- Use the reproducible provided on page 12 for students to complete and keep in their math notebooks or folders. Or, have students and parents sign it as a behavior contract at the beginning of the year. It may be helpful to preprogram the information before copying for students who need it.
- Review the anchor chart often in the first few weeks. Start reviewing it daily before beginning math workshop, and then gradually review it less often as students become more self-reliant.

Don't forget to **model, model, model!** Be sure to start slow, and practice will make perfect!

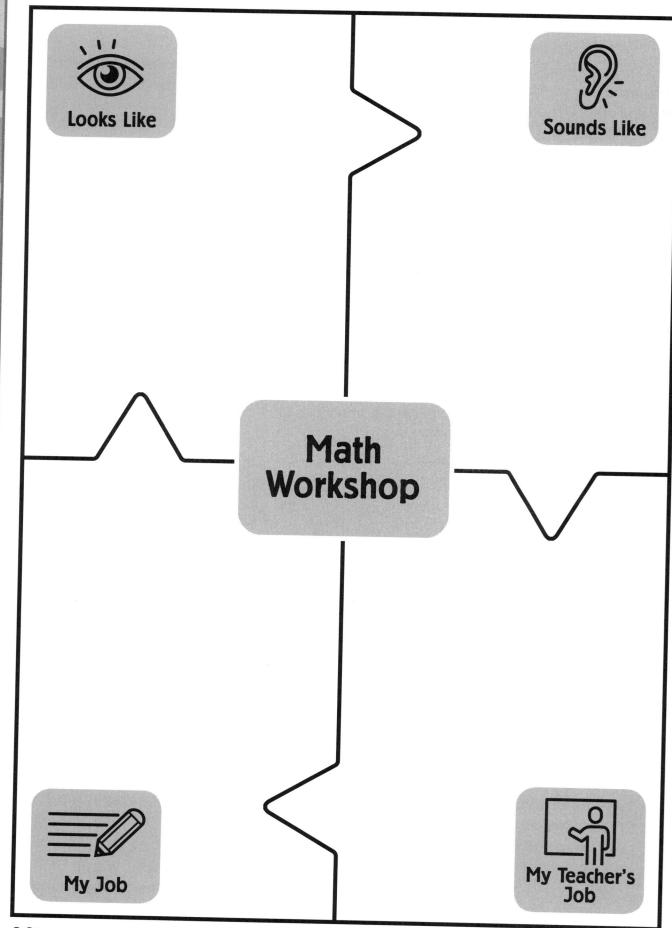

Looks Like

Sounds Like

Math Workshop

My Job

My Teacher's Job

Ensuring Accountability

While moving to a math workshop model has many benefits, it removes the traditional assessment and accountability options in the traditional teaching model. However, it's still necessary to prove in some way that students are working hard toward learning goals and making progress throughout the year. See the lists below for suggestions.

Accountability During Rotations

- Have students record their math thinking (for example, number sentences solved during a game) on whiteboards or something else that is highly visible. That way, you can see at a glance if students are working or not.
- Use activities with recording sheets that you can collect.
- Or, use a recording sheet where students record the rotations they visited and details about their work at each rotation.
- If desired, collect students' written work and/or recording sheets for a participation grade. Use the reproducible on page 14 as a weekly rotation recording sheet or create your own with the rotations specific to your math workshop (see example below).
- Initial, stamp, or sticker students' work daily. You can circulate and do this quickly during closure each day.
- Have students use a math journal to record their work during rotations.
- Utilize technology if possible—many programs and apps have built-in reports on the teacher side.

Assessment

- When not meeting with groups, use the guided math time to visit different stations and have students explain their math thinking for a quick formative assessment.
- During closure, use exit tickets. Use them as formative assessments, or keep them in a math notebook or portfolio to show progress.
- Designate one math workshop day a week or month for a more formal assessment that can be used for a grade or kept in portfolios.

Name_____   Date _____

Math Workshop

Mark off each rotation as you complete it. You must do seat work and technology every day!

Mon	Meet with Teacher	Seat Work	Technology	Fast Practice	Math Game
Tues	Meet with Teacher	Seat Work	Technology	Fast Practice	Math Game
Wed	Meet with Teacher	Seat Work	Technology	Fast Practice	Math Game

Math Rotations

Day	Rotation(s) Visited	Done?	Rate Yourself
Monday			
Tuesday			
Wednesday			
Thursday			
Friday			

1	2	3	4
I didn't do any work. I wasn't on task.	I didn't do my best work and was often off task.	I worked well, but was off task a little.	I worked hard and stayed on task.

Essential Question

How can you count to 100?

 Warm-Up/Review

Have students share about things in their lives that they can count. For example, *I count four people in my family. I count seven grapes in my bowl. I count two ears on my head.*

 Mini-Lesson

1. Have five students stand in a row at the front of the classroom. Tell the class that you are going to count the students. Explain that you are going to start with the number 1 when you point to the first student, followed by 2, 3, 4, and 5. Have the class repeat after you.

2. Next, have students sit in a circle. Have the first student say, "One" and continue to count the students around the circle. Help when needed.

3. Explain that when counting something such as people or other objects, they should always say the numbers in order.

4. Have students hold up their hands. Tell them that they can count their fingers. Have students practice counting from 1 to 10 on their fingers.

 Math Talk

If the same number of students changed where they were standing, would you count the same way? Why or why not?
Why is it important to start with the number 1?
Why do you need to say the numbers in order when you count?

 Journal Prompt

Draw a picture of or write the names of three things you can count in your room.

Materials

linking cubes
numbers 1–10 on large sheets of paper

 Workstations

Activity sheets (pages 17–19)
Counting by Ones Puzzles
(page 20)

 Guided Math

⬤ **Remediation: Counting by Ones to 5**

1. Have students gather in a circle and repeat the group counting activity from the mini-lesson (page 15). Have a student say, "One." Then, around the circle, each student should say the next number in the counting sequence. If desired, have students continue to say numbers around the circle until you say, "Stop."

2. Next, line up five linking cubes on the table. Point to one linking cube. Tell students that just like counting students, the linking cubes will help you count. Count aloud, "One, two, three, four, five."

3. Distribute five linking cubes to each student. Have students practice counting cubes 1 to 5. Students should rearrange and count again. Discuss how the count stays the same.

⬛ **On Level: Counting by Ones to 10**

1. Hold up one linking cube. Tell students that it is one object, so we count by saying, "One."

2. Now, place a second linking cube on top of the first one. Tell students that now there are two. Count aloud, "One, two."

3. Distribute 10 linking cubes to each student. Have students practice counting 1 to 10 by adding one linking cube each time.

4. Give each student a random amount (less than 10) of cubes and challenge students to count the sets.

▲ **Enrichment: The Counting Sequence**

1. Place 10 numbered sheets of paper facedown on the floor, forming a tower.

2. Have students take turns walking along the numbers and saying each number in the counting sequence. Point out that the higher the tower, the higher the number counted.

3. Turn over the sheets of paper and challenge students to arrange the numbers from left to right in counting order. Tell students that this is the basis for a number line. Explain that number lines can be used as a strategy for adding and subtracting.

 Assess and Extend

Have students tell what number they start with when counting. Students should explain why it is important to start with that number.

Counting

● Counting by Ones to 5

Count the cubes. Circle the number of cubes in each set.

1.   1   2   3

2.   2   3   4

3.   4   5   3

4.   1   2   3

5.   3   4   5

6.   4   5   6

★★3 Counting

Count the cubes. Circle the number of cubes in each set.

1.   6   7   8

2.   7   8   9

3.   7   8   9

4.   4   5   6

5.   4   5   6

⭐⭐⭐
★3 **Counting**   ▲ The Counting Sequence

Cut out the numbers. Glue the numbers in order in the boxes.
Say the numbers in order as you count them.

1			4	
		8		10
11			14	15
16		18		20

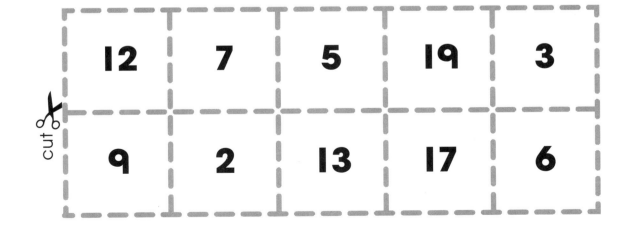

12	7	5	19	3
9	2	13	17	6

cut ✂

Counting by Ones Puzzles

Directions: Choose a puzzle. Put the numbers in order to make a picture.

To prep: Copy the puzzles on cardstock for durability. If desired, allow students to color the puzzles or use colored cardstock to create several sets. Cut apart the pieces and store the puzzles in resealable plastic bags or envelopes. Place them in a center with the directions.

Essential Question

How can you count to 100 by tens?

 Warm-Up/Review

Ask students to count aloud the number of fingers on two hands. Then, have all students count their fingers together while saying the numbers 1 to 10.

 Mini-Lesson

1. Have 10 students stand in a row with their hands outstretched, showing their fingers. Tell the class that you are going to count all of the fingers of the 10 students.

2. Begin counting by ones in one breath and fade out counting while acting exasperated. Say, "There must be a faster way."

3. Tell students that when counting a large group of something, it is easier to count by tens. Start with "ten" and count each students' fingers until you reach 100. Say, "That was a lot faster than counting by ones."

4. Have students form a circle. Have students count by tens to 100. Start over at 10 until every student has had a turn to say a number. Help as needed.

 Math Talk

How can you count the number of buttons on a shirt? Explain.

How can you count the number of buttons in a box of buttons? Explain.

Can you count by tens? Why or why not?

 Journal Prompt

Draw a picture of something you might count by tens.

Materials

straw bundles
hundred charts
transparent counters

 Workstations

Activity sheets (pages 23–25)
Counting by Tens Puzzles
(page 26)
Counting by Ones Puzzles
(page 20)

 Guided Math

◯ **Remediation: Counting by Tens to 50**
1. Have students place their outstretched hands in front of them. Tell them that you want to count all of their fingers, but there must be a faster way than counting by ones. Have students suggest ideas.
2. Model how to count by tens to 50. Say aloud each number slowly as you point to each student's hands.
3. Have students repeat the process, saying aloud each number.
4. Give each student a different amount of straw bundles (ten straws in each bundle). Have students place the bundles in rows. Have them practice counting by tens as they count the bundles.

▢ **On Level: Counting by Tens to 100**
1. Place 10 straw bundles in a row. Tell students that just like counting sets of 10 fingers, you will count sets of 10 straws.
2. Model counting by tens as you point to each straw bundle.
3. Give each student a different amount of straw bundles. Have students place the bundles in rows. Students should practice counting by tens as they count the bundles.

△ **Enrichment: Using a Hundred Chart**
1. Give each student a hundred chart and some transparent counters.
2. Have students place a counter on each number they count by ones from 1 to 10. Then, have students place a counter on each number they count by tens from 10 to 100.
3. Have students look at the numbers that are covered with counters. Ask students to share what they notice. Tell them that the same numbers they count 1 to 10 are the first part, or digits, of the numbers they count 10 to 100. (1, 10; 2, 20; 3, 30; etc.) Have students remove the counters from 1 to 9.
4. Next, have students place the counters on 5 and 10, and every number in the same columns. Have students count aloud the numbers starting at 5. Tell students that they counted by fives and that this is another way to count groups.
5. Challenge students to find another way to count other than ones, fives, or tens. Then, have students share their ways with the group.

 Assess and Extend

Count aloud several times by ones and tens, stopping at different ending numbers. Have students raise one finger each (or all 10 fingers) to show how you were counting.

Name ______________________ Date ______________

Counting by Tens

● Counting by Tens to 50

Cut out the numbers. Glue them into the correct boxes.

1. 10, 20, ☐, 40, 50

2. 10, 20, 30, 40, ☐

3. 10, ☐, 30, 40, 50

4. ☐, 20, 30, 40, 50

5. 10, 20, 30, ☐, 50

cut

10	20	30	40	50

3 **Counting by Tens**   Counting by Tens to 100

Cut out the numbers. Glue them into the correct boxes.

1. 10, 20, 30, 40, ▢

2. 20, ▢, 40, 50, 60

3. 30, ▢, 50, 60, 70

4. 40, 50, 60, 70, ▢

5. ▢, 70, 80, 90, 100

✂ cut | **80** | **40** | **30** | **50** | **60** |

⭐⭐⭐ Counting by Tens ▲ Using a Hundred Chart

1. Color the numbers you say when you count by ones to 10 yellow.

2. Color the numbers you say when you count by tens to 100 red.

3. Color the numbers you say when you count by fives to 100 blue.

1	2	3	4	5	6	7	8	9	10
11	12	13	14	15	16	17	18	19	20
21	22	23	24	25	26	27	28	29	30
31	32	33	34	35	36	37	38	39	40
41	42	43	44	45	46	47	48	49	50
51	52	53	54	55	56	57	58	59	60
61	62	63	64	65	66	67	68	69	70
71	72	73	74	75	76	77	78	79	80
81	82	83	84	85	86	87	88	89	90
91	92	93	94	95	96	97	98	99	100

Write one thing you notice about the numbers.

_____

_____

Counting by Tens Puzzles

Directions: Choose a puzzle. Put the numbers in order to make a picture.

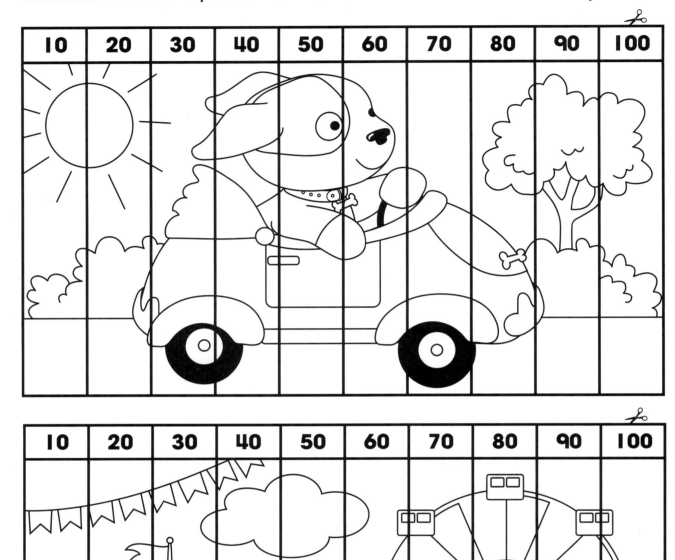

10	20	30	40	50	60	70	80	90	100

10	20	30	40	50	60	70	80	90	100

To prep: Copy the puzzles on cardstock for durability. If desired, allow students to color the puzzles or use colored cardstock to create several sets. Cut apart the pieces and store the puzzles in resealable plastic bags or envelopes. Place them in a center with the directions.

Essential Question

How does understanding the sequence of numbers help with counting on?

 Warm-Up/Review

Remind students that they have learned to count by ones. As a class, count from 1 to 10. Remind students that they have also learned to count by tens to 100. Count from 10 to 100 as a class.

 Mini-Lesson

Materials: coins

1. Tell students that you want to count some coins that you have. You know that you have two in your pocket and some in your hand. Tell students that because you already know what is in your pocket, you can just say, "two" and count the rest of the coins in your hand by counting aloud, "three, four, five."

2. Have students form a circle. Choose a student to be "4." Have the other students count on from 4 until the counting sequence comes back to the student who is "4". Repeat with other numbers such as 12, 25, 56, and 71. Help as needed.

3. Have students turn to partners and challenge them to count on from a number other than 1. Have them switch and repeat.

 Math Talk

How can you count on from this number?
Explain why counting on from this number is harder than the number ___?
How can you count back from this number?

 Journal Prompt

Explain how counting on makes counting easier.

Materials

twenty charts
hundred charts
blank 0–20 number lines
transparent counters

 Workstations

Activity sheets (pages 29–31)
Count On to Win (page 32)

 Guided Math

⬤ **Remediation: Counting On from a Number 2–9**

1. Have students count from 1 to 10. Then, tell students that you want them to count again, but instead of saying, "One," they should clap. Have students continue to replace the numbers with claps as they count to 10.
2. Explain that you can count from a number other than 1. Tell them that the counting sequence does not change; only the starting number changes.
3. Give each student a twenty chart and one counter. Tell students to drop their counters onto the charts. Then, each student should count on from the number her counter lands on to the end of the row.
4. Have students drop the counters and count on several times while you observe students' counting.

◼ **On Level: Counting On from a Number 10–99**

1. Give each student a hundred chart and one counter.
2. Model how to drop the counter and say aloud the number the counter lands on. Then, point to each number as you count on until the end of the row.
3. Have students drop and count on several times while you observe students' counting.

▲ **Enrichment: Counting with a Number Line**

1. Give each student a blank number line. Show students how each hash mark on the line represents a number. Have them write the numbers 0 to 20 on their lines.
2. Give each student a transparent counter. Have students place the counters on the number 5. Tell them to count on 2 more and say the number. Repeat with other numbers and amounts to count on. Tell students that counting on will help them understand addition.
3. Then, have students place their counters on 10. Tell them to count back four. Repeat with other numbers and amounts to count back. Tell students that counting back will help them understand subtraction.

 Assess and Extend

Have students choose a number from 2 to 10. Then, have them count on five more.

Counting On   ● Counting On from a Number 2–9

Choose a playing card. Write the number. Count on. Write the next two numbers.

Note: Remove face cards and aces from a deck of playing cards.

I. _____   _____   _____

2. _____   _____   _____

3. _____   _____   _____

4. _____   _____   _____

5. _____   _____   _____

6. _____   _____   _____

7. _____   _____   _____

8. _____   _____   _____

9. _____   _____   _____

10. _____   _____   _____

⭐⭐⭐ Counting On ▪ Counting On from a Number 10–99

Roll two dice. Use the numbers rolled to write a two-digit number. Count on. Write the next four numbers.

1. _____ _____ _____ _____ _____

2. _____ _____ _____ _____ _____

3. _____ _____ _____ _____ _____

4. _____ _____ _____ _____ _____

5. _____ _____ _____ _____ _____

6. _____ _____ _____ _____ _____

7. _____ _____ _____ _____ _____

8. _____ _____ _____ _____ _____

9. _____ _____ _____ _____ _____

10. _____ _____ _____ _____ _____

★3 Counting On   ▲ Counting with a Number Line

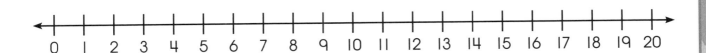

1. Use the number line to help you write the numbers that come **after**.

2	

15	

12	

6	

2. Use the number line to help you write the numbers that come **between**.

10		12

4		6

18		20

7		9

3. Use the number line to help you write the numbers that come **before**.

	8

	2

	14

	17

Count On to Win

Materials: number cube (1–3), game pieces

To play: Place the game pieces on 1. Players take turns. Roll the die and count on that many spaces. Count aloud as you move your game piece. The first player to reach the end wins.

1	2	3	4	5
6	7	8	9	10
11	12	13	14	15
16	17	18	19	20
21	22	23	24	25
26	27	28	29	30

Essential Question

How are the numbers 0 to 20 written? What does each number represent?

 Warm-Up/Review

Remind students that they have practiced counting by ones and tens. Say a number and have them count on three more numbers. Repeat with several other numbers.

 Mini-Lesson

Materials: dot cards 0–9, dry-erase boards and markers

1. Explain that students are going to learn how to write numbers to tell how many objects are in a set. Show them a dot card with one dot. Tell them that to find the number, they have to count the dots. Say, "Let's count *one*." Model how to write the number. Repeat with the remaining dot cards.

2. Give each student a dry-erase board and marker. Have students follow you as you write each number. Then, have them hold up the boards so you can observe which students are still having trouble. Have students use their fingers to trace and erase each number.

3. Repeat step 2 with the numbers 0 to 9 in a different order.

 Math Talk

What do you notice about the numbers 1 and 7? 6 and 9?
Which numbers have curves? Straight lines?
How are these two numbers the same? Different?

 Journal Prompt

Write the numbers 0 to 9.

Materials

dry-erase boards and markers
jumbo magnetic numbers (or
    cardstock number cutouts)
opaque cloth or paper bag
dot cards 0–9
number cards 0–20
20 counters in bags

 Workstations

Activity sheets (pages 35–37)
Number Puzzles (page 38)

 Guided Math

⬤ **Remediation: Writing Numbers**

1. Give each student a magnetic number. Have each student trace the number several times. Discuss which numbers have straight lines, which have curves, and which have both straight and curved lines.
2. Then, have students put their numbers into the bag. Have each student reach into the bag and try to find her number. Help as needed.
3. Switch numbers and repeat steps 1 and 2.
4. Give each student a dry-erase board and marker. Have students write each number as you demonstrate on your board. Have each student trace her number with one finger to erase.

▢ **On Level: Counting Sets and Writing Numbers**

1. Give each student a dry-erase board and marker.
2. Give each student a dot card. Have her count the number of dots and say the number. Then, have her write the number on her board.
3. Switch dot cards and repeat step 2.
4. Challenge each student to write a number and find the dot card that matches.

△ **Enrichment: Making Sets for Numbers**

1. Give each student a bag of at least 20 counters.
2. Have each student choose a number card. Have her show the number with a set of counters. Repeat several more times.
3. Challenge students to arrange the counters in an organized way such as in columns and rows, groups, etc.

 Assess and Extend

Challenge students to find and count sets within the classroom and label them with the numbers written on sticky notes.

Reading and Writing Numbers to 20 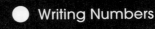 Writing Numbers

Trace. Count. Write.

1   _____

2  _____

3  _____

4  _____

5  _____

6  _____

7  _____

8  _____

9  _____

⭐⭐⭐ Reading and Writing Numbers to 20 ☐ Counting Sets and Writing Numbers

Count and write the number.

1.   _____

2.    _____

3.    _____

4.    _____

5. 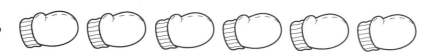   _____

6.    _____

★3 Reading and Writing Numbers to 20   ▲ Making Sets for Numbers

Draw a set of objects for each number.

8	4	7
6	2	9
3	5	1

Number Puzzles

Directions: Choose a bag. Join the matching numbers and sets.

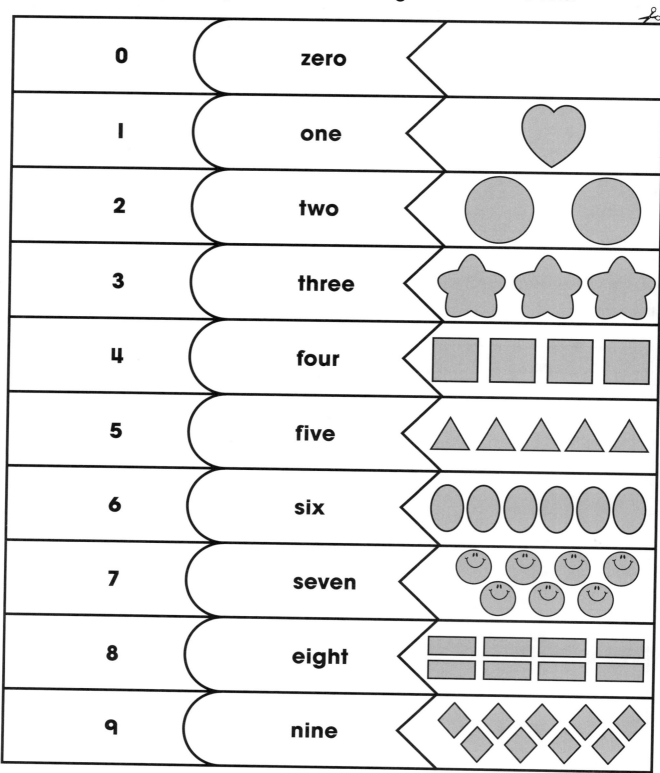

To prep: Copy multiple sets of the puzzles on different colors of cardstock for durability. Cut apart each set and store it in its own resealable plastic bag. Place the puzzles in a center with the directions.

Essential Question

Why is the last number you say when counting important?

Warm-Up/Review

Remind students that they have practiced counting and writing numbers. Have students count by ones to 10. Ask a volunteer to come to the board and write the numbers as the rest of the students count.

 Mini-Lesson

Materials: linking cubes

1. Have five students stand in a row at the front of the classroom. Have the rest of the class count the students aloud as you touch each student's shoulder. Write 5 on the board. Ask, "If we rearrange these students, will there still be five?" Encourage students to explain their reasoning.

2. Ask the volunteers to stand in a different order. Count again. Discuss the results. (The order of the students does not change the quantity.)

3. Give each student a set of seven linking cubes.

4. Ask, "How many cubes do you have?" Have students point to each cube as they count, mix the cubes, and count again. If students miscount, encourage them to link the cubes as they count so they do not "double count."

 Math Talk

How can you count these objects so that each one is counted only once?
Can you show these objects arranged in another way? Is the number of objects still the same?
Why does lining up the cubes make them easier to count?

 Journal Prompt

Explain how the number of objects does not change when they are moved around.

Materials

linking cubes
number cards 1–20

 Workstations

Activity sheets (pages 41–43)
Count and Dab (page 44)
Number Puzzles (page 38)

 Guided Math

◯ Remediation: Counting Objects in a Set

1. Give each student a set of five linking cubes. Ask, "How many cubes do you have?" Have students link their cubes and point to each cube as they count. Have them unlink, rearrange, link, and count again.
2. Display a number card and read the number to the group. Ask students to show that number by linking the cubes. Have students point and count aloud to check for accuracy. Repeat for each number.
3. Have each student show any number of cubes from 1 to 5 and then choose the number card that matches his set. Repeat if time allows.
4. Ask students to share something they know about counting. Use the discussion as an opportunity to reinforce that the order of the objects does not change the quantity.

▢ On Level: Matching Sets and Numbers

1. Give each student a set of 10 linking cubes. Ask, "How many cubes do you have?" Observe counting strategies and help as needed.
2. Display a number card and ask students to identify the number. Have students show that number with their cubes (linked or unlinked). Repeat for each number 1 to 10. If students miscount, encourage them to link the cubes so that they do not "double count."
3. Lay the cards facedown on the table. Place a set of linking cubes for each number on the table. Challenge students to work together to match the numbers and sets.

▲ Enrichment: Building Sets

1. Give each student a set of 20 linking cubes and a set of number cards.
2. Say any number 10 to 20. Have students find the number card and build matching sets with the cubes. Repeat with several numbers from 10 to 20.
3. Place one set of the number cards 10 to 20 faceup on the table. Challenge students to work together to arrange the numbers in order. Then, have students use their cubes to make matching sets for each number.

 Assess and Extend

Have students draw 6 objects. Then, have students label each object with a number as they count. Students should also circle the number that tells how many.

3 **Connecting Counting to Quantity** ●

Count and write the number. Draw a set to match.

1.  _____

2.  _____

3.  _____

4.  _____

5. _____

⭐⭐⭐ Connecting Counting to Quantity

Color the fruit to match the number on each tree.

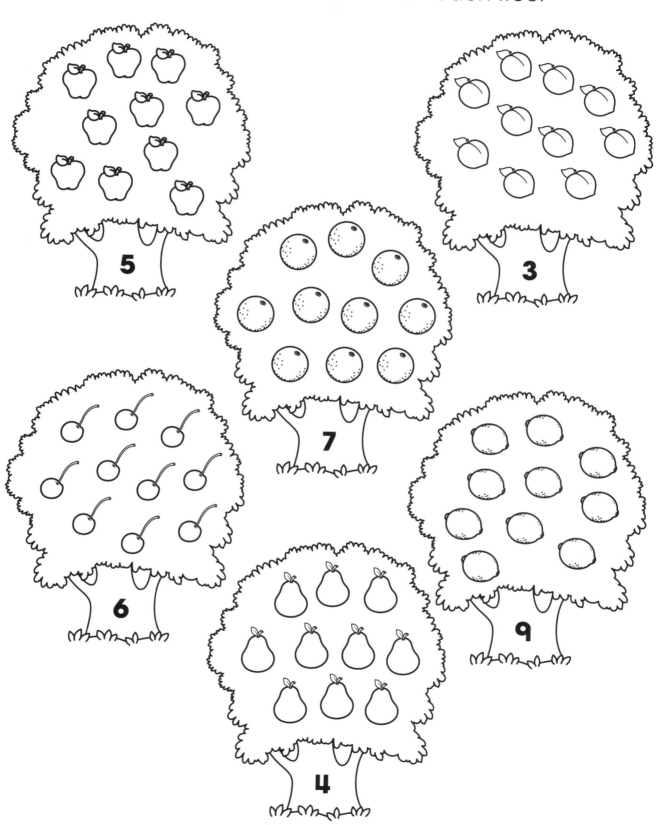

3 | **Connecting Counting to Quantity**   ▲ Building Sets

Draw a set of objects to match each number.

12	18
16	**11**
14	**15**

Count and Dab

Materials: dot or bingo markers
Directions: Dab each pet as you count. Write the number.

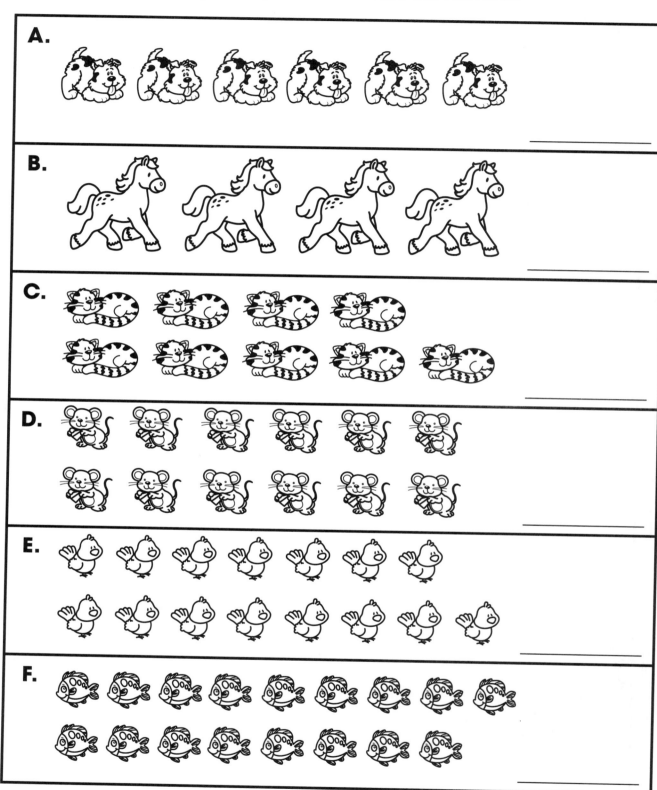

A. _____

B. _____

C. _____

D. _____

E. _____

F. _____

To prep: Make several copies of the worksheet. If desired, copy on cardstock and cut along the solid lines to create strips for students to choose from. Place the worksheets or strips in a center with the materials and directions.

Counting Sets

 Essential Question

How does counting tell how many?

Warm-Up/Review

Have students share the methods they use to count things, such as pointing to each object or moving each object from a set as they count. Have volunteers demonstrate each method.

 Mini-Lesson

Materials: ten frames, counters, ten frame models (1–10)

1. Explain how students can use a tool called a *ten frame* to help them count how many objects are in a set. Display the ten frame and tell students that it is called a ten frame because it has 10 boxes in all and five boxes in each row.

2. Show students one counter. Model how to place the counter in the ten frame (from top to bottom and left to right). Continue with 2, 3, 4, etc.

3. Display models of each ten frame. Point out that each ten frame's picture shows a set that represents only one number 1 to 10. For example, students should know that a full row is 5, and a full row plus 1 box in the next row is 6.

4. Give each student a ten frame and 10 counters. Say a number. Have students place the counters in their ten frames to match. Observe and make corrections as needed.

 Math Talk

Where would you place the counters to show this number?

Where do you start placing the counters on the ten frame?

What if you have more counters than will fit on the ten frame?

 Journal Prompt

Explain how a ten frame (five frame, double ten frame) helps tell how many.

Materials

five frames
counters
number cards 1–20
index cards
ten frames
double ten frames

 Workstations

Activity sheets (pages 47–49)
Count and Clip (page 50)
Count and Dab (page 44)
Number Puzzles (page 38)

 Guided Math

○ **Remediation: Using a Five Frame to Count to 5**

1. Give each student a five frame and five counters. Have students place one counter in each box until their five frames are full. Emphasize one-to-one correspondence between the numbers and the counters.
2. Display a number card 1 to 5. Have students say the number aloud. Then, have them place the counters on their frames to show the number. Encourage students to count quietly as they count on to that number. Repeat with the remaining numbers.
3. Challenge students to make each number again and write the numbers on index cards.

▢ **On Level: Using a Ten Frame to Count to 10**

1. Give each student a ten frame and 10 counters. Have students place one counter in each box until their ten frames are full. Emphasize one-to-one correspondence between the numbers and the counters.
2. Display a number card 1 to 10. Have students say the number aloud. Then, have them place the counters on their ten frames to show the number. Encourage students to count quietly as they count on to that number. Repeat with the remaining numbers.
3. Give each student a random amount of counters from 1 to 10. Display the number cards 1 to 10. Have each student use a ten frame to count his set and find the number card that matches it.

▲ **Enrichment: Using a Double Ten Frame to Count to 20**

1. Give each student a double ten frame and 20 counters. Have students place one counter in each box until the ten frames are full.
2. Display a number card 11 to 20. Have students say the number aloud. Then, have students place the counters on their frames to show the number. Encourage students to count quietly as they count on to that number. Repeat with the remaining numbers.
3. Give each student a random amount of counters from 11 to 20. Display the number cards 11 to 20. Have each student count her set and find the number card that matches it. Discuss how they can count on from 10 because they know the full ten frame shows 10.

 Assess and Extend

Have each student draw a ten frame. Then, have students show the number 8 with dots. Students should explain how they placed the dots in the ten frames.

⭐⭐⭐ Counting Sets   ⬤ Using a Five Frame to Count to 5

1. Draw a dot in the frame to match each number.

2

1

3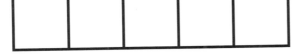

5

4

2. Write the number for each set.

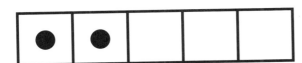   _____

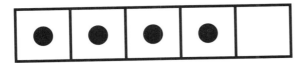   _____

   _____

3 **Counting Sets** | Using a Ten Frame to Count to 10

1. Fill in the ten frame for each number.

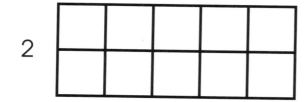 2

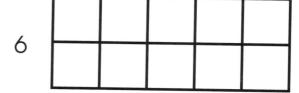 6

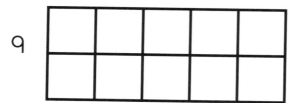 9

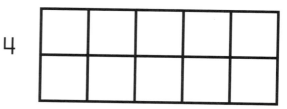 4

2. Count each set. Circle the ten frame that matches it.

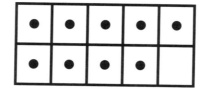

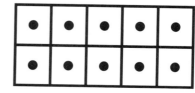

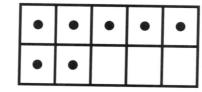

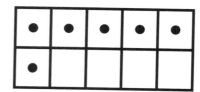

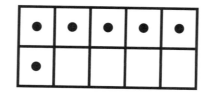

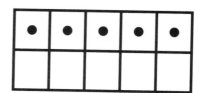

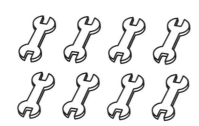

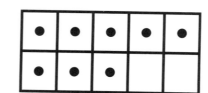

Name _____

Date _____

⭐⭐⭐ Counting Sets ▲ Using a Double Ten Frame to Count to 20

1. Fill in the ten frames for each number.

12

19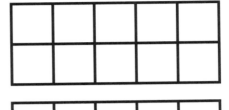

11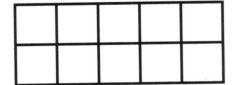

14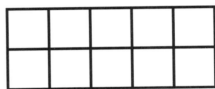

2. Count each set. Circle the set of ten frames that match.

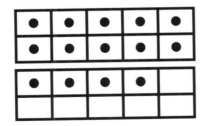

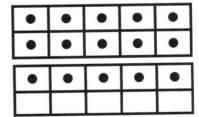

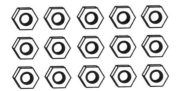

49

Count and Clip

Materials: clothespins

Directions: Tell how many are on each ten frame. Clip a clothespin to the number that matches. Turn over the card to check the answer.

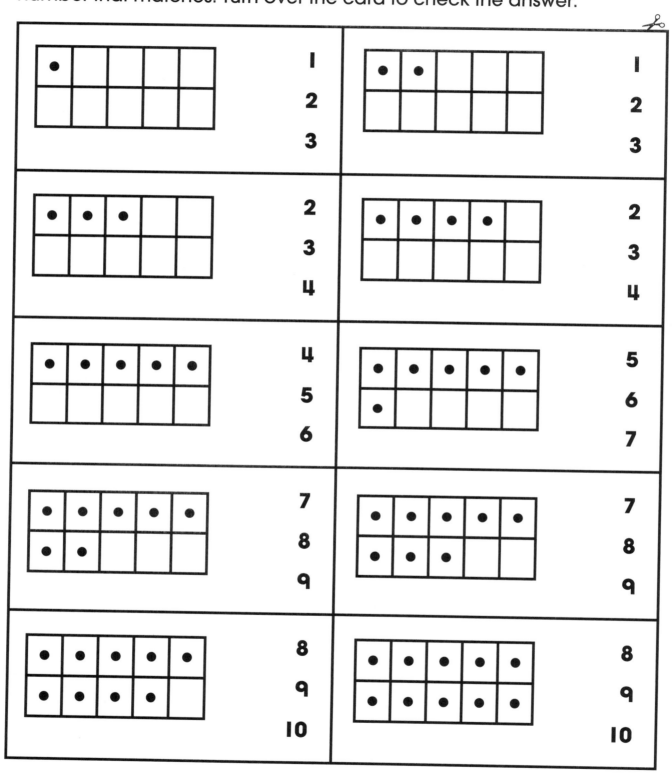

To prep: Copy on cardstock. Cut out the cards. Place a dot on the back of each card where the correct number would be clipped. Place the cards in a center with the materials and directions.

Essential Question

How can two groups of objects be compared?

 Warm-Up/Review

Ask students to think about a time when they compared how many candies they had to how many candies siblings or friends had. Have students share how they knew the other people had more or less.

 Mini-Lesson

Materials: linking cubes

1. Invite four students to stand as a group on one side of the classroom and six students to stand on the other side.

2. Have the remaining students count the students in each group and determine which group has more (*greater than*) and which has fewer (*less than*).

3. Model how to compare the two groups. Say, "This group has less than that group. This group has more than that group." Encourage students to describe their strategies such as "I counted four and six. I know that four is less than six." or "I lined up the groups and matched the students one to one. I could see that the group of six is longer or greater than the group of four."

4. Repeat steps 1 and 2 several times with different numbers of students.

5. Give students different amounts of linking cubes. Have students link the cubes and compare their sets with students next to them. Have them use *more* and *less* to describe how their sets compare.

 Math Talk

How does lining up the groups help you see that one group is more or less?

How many more students need to move to this side to make both groups the same, or equal?

How much greater is one group than the other group?

 Journal Prompt

Draw or write about how you would find out if your class has more boys or more girls.

Materials

small paper plates
counters
dice

 Workstations

Activity sheets (pages 53–55)
Roll and Compare (page 56)

 Guided Math

⬤ Remediation: More or Less

1. Give each student two plates and 10 counters.
2. Have students place three counters on one plate and two counters on the other plate.
3. Ask, "Which plate has more?" or "Which plate has less?" Have students share their answers and tell how they know.
4. Repeat with increasingly larger sets up to 10.

▢ On Level: Greater Than, Less Than, or Equal To

1. Introduce the concept of *equal* as having the same amount. Place four counters each on two paper plates. Ask, "What do you notice about the counters on the paper plates?" Ask students to count with you aloud as you count the first group of four. Then, count the second paper plate of four counters aloud. Say, "These two plates have the same amount of counters on them so they are equal." Have students take turns placing equal amounts of counters on the paper plates.
2. Give each pair of students two small paper plates, 12 counters, and one die. Model rolling the die and placing that number of counters on one plate. Roll again and place that number of counters on the other plate. Ask students, "Which plate has more counters? Less counters? Are any sets the same, or equal?"
3. With partners, have students take turns rolling a die and placing their counters on the plates. Partners should ask each other the questions as modeled in step 2.

▲ Enrichment: Making Sets Equal

1. Review the concept of equal.
2. Give each student two paper plates, 18 counters, and one die. Model rolling the die and placing the rolled number of counters on one plate. Roll again and place that number of counters on the other plate. Ask students, "Which plate has more counters? Less counters? Are any sets the same, or equal?
3. Have students practice rolling their dice, placing their counters on the plates, and comparing the sets.
4. Then, challenge students to find out how many counters they need to remove from the plates that have more counters so that the groups are equal. Encourage students to share their answers and strategies.

 Assess and Extend

Draw two sets of objects of different amounts. Have students tell you which set has more. Draw another set of objects. Have students tell you which set has less.

3 | **Comparing Sets**　　　　　　　　　　　● More or Less

Color the set that has more.

1.　　　　　　　　　

2.　　　

3.　　　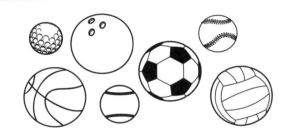

4.　　　

5.　　　

★★★3 Comparing Sets ▢ Greater Than, Less Than, or Equal To

Count the objects in the first set. Color the set that is greater red. Color the set that is less yellow. Color the set that is the same, or equal, blue.

1.

2.

3.

4.

5.

3 ## Comparing Sets   ▲ Making Sets Equal

Count the objects in each set. Circle the set that has more.
Draw **X**s on objects in that set to make both sets the same, or
equal.

1. ◯ ◯ ◯ ◯   ◯ ◯ ◯

2.

3.

4.

5.

Roll and Compare

Materials: 1 or 2 dice, crayons

To play: Each player rolls a die. The player with the greatest set of dots colors a square. If players roll equal numbers, roll again. The player who colors all of his squares first wins.

Round 1

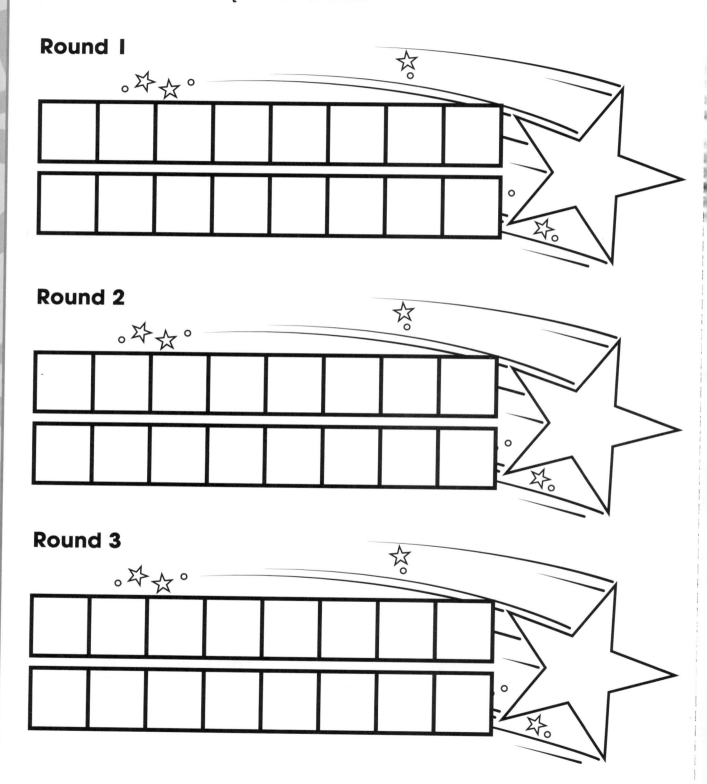

Round 2

Round 3

Comparing Numbers

 Essential Question

How can numbers 1 to 10 be compared?

 Warm-Up/Review

Remind students that to compare sets of objects to find out which set has more or less (*greater than* or *less than*), they can line up the objects and match them one to one. Or, they can count the sets and use what they know about numbers to compare the sets.

 Mini-Lesson

Materials: small sticky notes, individual number lines numbered 0 to 10, transparent counters

1. Display a large number line 0 to 10. Give each student two or three sticky notes (for a total of 55). Model how to place a sticky note above the number 1 on the number line. Have each student come to the board and place a sticky note above one number. Once the number of sticky notes is equal to the number, students can no longer place sticky notes above it.

2. Have students observe the pattern of notes above the numbers. Ask, "What do you notice?" Explain that as the counting sequence moves toward 10, the set for each number is taller, or greater.

3. Tell students, "We can use a number line to help compare numbers." Give each student a number line and two transparent counters. Write two numbers on the board. Have students place the counters on each number. Then, have students compare the numbers using vocabulary such as *greater than* or *less than*. Repeat several times with different pairs of numbers.

 Math Talk

How do you know that this number is greater than that number?
How do you know that this number is less than that number?
How much more or less is this number than that number?

 Journal Prompt

How do you know if a number is more or less than another number? Explain the strategies you could use to find out.

Materials

linking cubes
number cards 1–20
comparison symbol cards

 Workstations

Activity sheets (pages 59–61)
Greater Number Clip
   (page 62)
Roll and Compare (page 56)

 Guided Math

○ Remediation: Comparing Numbers 1–5

1. Give each student a set of 15 linking cubes. Have students make towers of 1 cube, 2 cubes, 3 cubes, 4 cubes, and 5 cubes. Have them line up the towers along the bottoms. Ask, "What do you notice about the towers?" Then, explain that as you count on, the numbers become greater.

2. Give each student two number cards 1 to 5. Have each student use the cubes to build a tower for each number. Model how to compare the numbers by placing them side by side. Have each student tell which number is greater and which number is less by looking at the heights of the towers.

3. Give each student one number card. Challenge her to find another student who has a number that is more and a number that is less than hers.

▢ On Level: Comparing Numbers 1–10

1. Give each student a set of 20 linking cubes and two number cards 1 to 10. Have each student use the cubes to build a tower for each number.

2. Model how to compare the numbers by placing them side by side. Have each student tell which number is greater and which number is less by looking at the heights of the towers.

3. Switch cards and repeat.

4. Challenge each student to find another student who has one number that is more and one number that is less than his.

△ Enrichment: Comparing Numbers 11–19

1. Give each student a set of 40 linking cubes, two number cards 11 to 19, and a comparison symbol card (<). Have each student use the cubes to build a tower for each number. Encourage students to build towers only as tall as 10 and then begin new towers with the remaining cubes. This will help establish the placement of tens and ones during future place value lessons.

2. Model how to compare the numbers by placing the towers side by side. Have each student tell which number is greater and which number is less by looking at the heights of the towers. Then, say, "I think this symbol looks like an alligator's mouth. An alligator is hungry and would eat the bigger meal. Let's put the alligator mouth opening toward the bigger set. The set the alligator wants to eat is greater than the other set." Have a student "read" his comparison by telling the numbers and using *greater than* or *less than*. Explain that students can turn the symbol card to point to the other side, as long as the alligator's mouth is still open to the greater number.

3. Challenge each student to find another student who has a number that is more and a number that is less than hers.

 Assess and Extend

Have students write two numbers and draw a set for each. Students should then circle the greater number and set.

★3 Comparing Numbers   ● Comparing Numbers 1–5

Color the number that is more.

     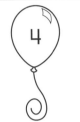

Comparing Numbers

Color the number that is more.

Comparing Numbers   ▲ Comparing Numbers 11–19

Write > or < to compare each set of numbers.

1. 11 ◯ 14   14 ◯ 15   17 ◯ 13

2. 16 ◯ 18   17 ◯ 12   13 ◯ 19

3. 12 ◯ 14   15 ◯ 16   18 ◯ 13

4. 19 ◯ 17   12 ◯ 18   14 ◯ 16

5. 18 ◯ 17   19 ◯ 12   11 ◯ 17

Greater Number Clip

Materials: clothespins

Directions: Choose a card. Compare the numbers. Clip a clothespin to the greater number. Turn over the card to check the answer.

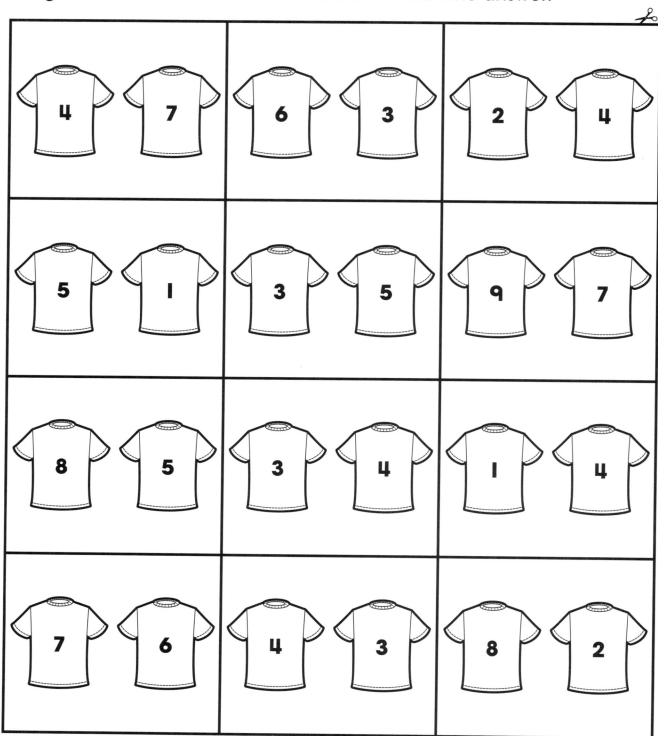

To prep: Copy on cardstock and laminate for durability. Cut apart the cards. Place a dot on the back of each side with the greater number. Place the cards in a center with the materials and directions.

Understanding Addition

 Essential Question

What are some different ways to add?

 Warm-Up/Review

Have students hold up their left hands if they agree they show five fingers. Have students hold up their right hands if they agree they show five fingers. Have students put their hands close together and wiggle them if they agree that they have a greater set of fingers when their hands are put together.

 Mini-Lesson

Materials: document camera or overhead projector, counters

1. Use a document camera or overhead projector to model combining to get more. Place 2 counters on the left and 2 on the right. Have students count each set with you.

2. Say, "I wonder how many counters I will have if I put the sets of counters together." Move the counters to the center and count again. Then, explain, "I had 2 over here and 2 over here, and now I have 4 altogether."

3. Follow the same steps with 3 counters on the left and 3 counters on the right, 2 counters on the left and 3 counters on the right, and 5 counters on the left and 2 counters on the right.

4. Use the words *add*, *more*, *in all*, and *altogether* as you work through each example.

5. Give each student 10 counters. Have students practice making small sets and combining the sets to make larger sets.

 Math Talk

How did you make that number?
Can you make that number another way?
What happens to the number when you put sets together?
What do you notice about the total number of counters?

 Journal Prompt

For the numbers 1 to 10, which number will have the least amount of addition combinations? Most combinations? Explain.

Materials

linking cubes
dry-erase boards
dry-erase markers

 Workstations

Activity sheets (pages 65–67)
Addition Four-in-a-Row (page 68)

 Guided Math

◯ **Remediation: Combining Sets to 5**

1. Give each student 10 linking cubes (5 of one color and 5 of another).
2. Model combining cubes to make sums to 7. Say, for example, "If I have 1 red cube, and I add 3 blue cubes, I have 4 cubes in all." Be sure to represent each value with a different color.
3. Allow students time to explore this concept independently and encourage them to think aloud as they work. Ask questions such as, "How did you make 3?"
4. Challenge students to think of at least two different ways to make 4 and 5. Have students show and explain what they did with the cubes.

▢ **On Level: Combining Sets to 10**

1. Give each student 20 linking cubes (10 of one color and 10 of another).
2. Guide students through the process of combining cubes to make sums to 10. Say, for example, "If I have 4 red cubes, and I add 2 blue cubes, I have 6 cubes in all." Be sure that each value is represented by a different color.
3. Allow students time to explore this concept independently and encourage them to think aloud as they work. Ask questions such as, "How did you make 7?"
4. Challenge students to think of at least three different ways to make 6, 7, 8, and 9. Have students show and explain what they did with the cubes.

▲ **Enrichment: Writing Number Sentences**

1. Give each student 20 linking cubes (10 of one color and 10 of another) and dry-erase boards and markers.
2. Tell students that they will explore combining sets to 20.
3. Allow students time to explore this concept independently and encourage them to think aloud as they work. Ask questions such as, "How did you make 12?"
4. Model how to read and write addition number sentences. Show students a linked set of 6 red cubes and 4 blue cubes. Write *6 and 4 is 10* and *6 + 4 = 10*.
5. Challenge students to find all of the addition combinations for the numbers 11 and 12. Have students record the combinations on their boards as number sentences using numerals, words, and/or symbols.

 Assess and Extend

Have students draw a set of dots on the left and a set of dots on the right. Students should count and write the number of dots in all.

Understanding Addition ● Combining Sets to 5

Use two colors to color the pictures. Write the numbers.

1.

_____ and _____ make 5.

2.

_____ and _____ make 5.

3.

_____ and _____ make 5.

4.

_____ and _____ make 5.

Understanding Addition

Use two colors to color the cubes in different ways. Write the numbers.

1.

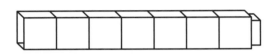

_____ and _____ make _____.

2.

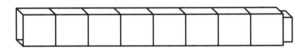

_____ and _____ make _____.

3.

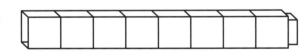

_____ and _____ make _____.

4.

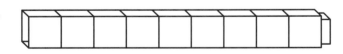

_____ and _____ make _____.

5.

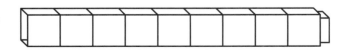

_____ and _____ make _____.

6.

_____ and _____ make _____.

➕➖➗✖ Understanding Addition   ▲ Writing Number Sentences

Look at the pictures. Write the numbers to complete the number sentences.

1.

_____ + _____ = 6

2.

_____ + _____ = 8

3.

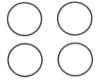   

_____ + _____ = 9

4.

_____ + _____ = 10

5. Choose a number sentence above. Write another number sentence that is equal to the same number.

_____ + _____ = _____

Addition Four-in-a-Row

Materials: number cubes (0–5), two colors of dry-erase markers

To play: Players take turns. Roll the number cubes. Add the numbers and color the sum on the game board. If a player rolls a sum that is already colored, she loses a turn. The first player to color four boxes in a row, column, or diagonally wins.

4	7	2	9	2	8
0	10	7	3	5	1
6	8	1	10	7	5
1	2	4	8	4	7
3	10	5	6	6	0
7	9	3	9	7	6
4	6	7	5	8	3

To prep: Copy on card stock and for durability laminate so students can use dry-erase markers. Place the game board in a center with the materials and directions. Cut off these directions before copying.

Understanding Subtraction

 Essential Question

What are some different ways to subtract?

 Warm-Up/Review

Ask students to think about when they go to PE. Ask, "What happens to the class when the PE teacher puts you on teams to play a game?" (We separate into smaller groups.) "Are the two groups smaller or larger than when we were together?" (They are smaller.) Tell students that they will learn how to separate sets and numbers to make smaller sets and numbers.

 Mini-Lesson

Materials: counters

1. Have five students come to the front of the classroom. Ask the remaining students to tell how many are in the set. Tell the class to pretend that two students have to go to get water. Have two students return to their seats.

2. Ask students to describe what happened to the original set. (It became smaller. It is less.)

3. Next, model how you would tell what happened as a subtraction problem. Say, "There were 5 students. Two students had to go to get water. Now, there are 3 students left over. I can separate 5 into 3 and 2." Draw a number bond to demonstrate the relationship.

4. Repeat with another set of students and ask a volunteer to describe what happened.

5. Use the words *subtract*, *take away*, and *left over* as you work through each example.

6. Give each student 10 counters. Have each student practice separating a number of counters from the set and describing to a partner what happened. Encourage students to use numbers and subtraction vocabulary to describe what happened.

 Math Talk

If you separate this set into two smaller sets, what would the numbers be?
What numbers can you use to describe what happened in this separation?
How did you separate this set?

 Journal Prompt

Explain why an answer in a subtraction problem is less than the starting number. How is this different from what you do in an addition problem?

Materials

linking cubes
cups
two-color counters

 Workstations

Activity sheets (pages 71–73)
Roll and Remove (page 74)

Guided Math

● Remediation: Decomposing Sets

1. Give each student seven linking cubes. Have students count the cubes as they link them together. Ask students to tell how many in all.
2. Next, model how to pick up the linked cubes by the ends (like holding an ear of corn). Ask students to "break" their cube trains into two pieces. Model how to count each piece, or smaller set, and use numbers to describe what happened. Say, for example, "I had 7 cubes. I broke, or separated, 7 cubes into 3 cubes and 4 cubes."
3. Have students relink their cubes and break the cube trains again. Have students compare their pieces to the students next to them. Have students share what they notice. (I have two smaller pieces. I have the same number in each piece as he does. I have different sized pieces than she does. We both started with the same amount.)

■ On Level: Subtracting from a Number

1. Give each student a cup and 10 two-color counters. Model how to carefully pour out the counters, line up the counters by like color, and count how many of each color you get. Say, for example, "I have 6 red and 3 yellow."
2. Have students pour out their counters, line up the counters by like color, and count how many of each color they get.
3. Tell students to return all of the yellow counters to the cups. Model how to take away the counters and how to describe what happens to the set. Say, for example, "I have 10 counters. I take away 3 yellow counters. I have 7 red counters left. 10 take away 3 is 7."
4. Have students practice pouring out counters and describing to partners how they take away the yellow counters and find what is left. Explain that subtraction is separating, or taking away, a smaller set from a larger set.

▲ Enrichment: Writing Number Sentences

1. Give each student a cup and 10 two-color counters. Model how to carefully pour out the counters, line up the counters by like color, and count how many of each color you get.
2. Tell students that they will explore separating sets and writing number sentences and describe what they did. Have students pour out their counters, line up the counters by like color, and count how many of each color they get.
3. Tell students to return all of the yellow counters to the cups. Model how to describe what happens to the set using a number sentence. Tell students that the symbol for "take away" is a minus sign, and the symbol for "same as" is the equal sign. Say, for example, "I have 10 counters. take away 6 yellow counters. I have 4 red counters left. 10 take away 6 is 4. $10 - 6 = 4$."
4. Allow students time to explore this concept independently and encourage them to think aloud as they work. Have students record the separations on their papers using numerals, words, and/or symbols in subtraction number sentences.

Assess and Extend

Have students draw pictures of 8 cookies. Say, "You had 8 cookies. You ate 4 cookies. How many do you have left?" Have students draw an X on each cookie they ate and write the number to show what they have left.

Name _____ Date _____

Understanding Subtraction

 Decomposing Sets

Look at each set. Write the number that is left.

1. 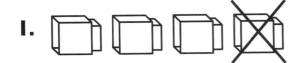   4 take away 1 is _____

2.    5 take away 2 is _____

3.    3 take away 0 is _____

4. 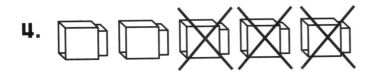   5 take away 3 is _____

5. 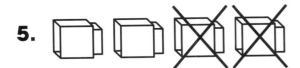   4 take away 2 is _____

Understanding Subtraction

Draw an **X** on each object taken away. Write the number that is left.

1. 6 take away 3 is _____

2. 7 take away 4 is _____

3. 4 take away 1 is _____

4. 5 take away 4 is _____

5. 8 take away 2 is _____

6. 9 take away 3 is _____

Name_____   Date _____

Understanding Subtraction   ▲ Writing Number Sentences

Write the number sentence for each picture.

1.

_____ – _____ = _____

2.

_____ – _____ = _____

3.

_____ – _____ = _____

4.

_____ – _____ = _____

5.

_____ – _____ = _____

6.

_____ – _____ = _____

Roll and Remove

Materials: 2 dice or 2 sets of dot cards 1–6, counters

To play: Players cover their cookies with counters. Players take turns. Roll the dice (or draw two cards) and subtract the numbers to get an answer. Remove that many counters from your board. The first player to clear his board wins.

Player 1

Player 2

Addition Word Problems

Essential Question

How can objects and pictures be used to show a problem?

Warm-Up/Review

Ask some students to come to the front of the room. Then, ask a few more. Tell students that you are doing addition. Ask the remaining students to come to the front of the room. Remind students that when you combine, or join groups of objects (or people in this case), you are adding.

★ Mini-Lesson

Materials: sheets of green paper, red counters

1. Give each student a sheet of green paper and 10 red counters. Tell students that the green paper is a leaf, and the red counters are ladybugs.

2. Say, "Two ladybugs are sitting on a leaf. Three more ladybugs join them. How many ladybugs are sitting on the leaf in all?" Tell students that you are going to read the story again and model how to place the ladybugs on the leaf. Tell them to follow along with you and place their counters as well. Say, "Two ladybugs are sitting on a leaf." Place 2 red counters on the paper. Say, "Three more ladybugs join them." Place 3 red counters on the paper. Then, say, "How many ladybugs are on the leaf in all?" Line up the counters and count aloud, "1, 2, 3, 4, 5. There are 5 ladybugs in all."

3. Tell students another ladybug story problem and place the counters on the paper. Repeat the story problem two more times with different combinations.

Math Talk

How many objects did you start with?
How many objects did you add to the first set?
How many objects do you have in all?

Journal Prompt

Draw a leaf that has 3 ladybugs and 1 more ladybug. Write the number that tells how many ladybugs in all.

Materials

sheets of blue paper (or fishbowl pictures)
orange counters
dry-erase boards
dry-erase markers

 Workstations

Activity sheets (pages 77–79)
Addition Story Problem Task Cards (page 80)

 Guided Math

◯ Remediation: Solving with Objects

1. Give each student a sheet of blue paper (or fishbowl picture) and 10 orange counters. Tell students that the blue paper is water, and the counters are fish.
2. Model how to use the counters to act out a story problem. Say, "Two fish are swimming in the water." Place 2 orange counters on the paper. "Two more fish join them." Place 2 more counters on the paper. "How many fish are in the water in all?" Line up the counters and count aloud, "1, 2, 3, 4. There are 4 fish in all."
3. Tell students another story problem and place the counters on the paper. Repeat step 2 two more times with different combinations.

▢ On Level: Solving with Pictures

1. Give yourself and each student a dry-erase board and marker. Tell students that you are going to tell them a story problem and show them how to draw pictures to solve the problem.
2. Say, "Two fish are swimming in the water." Draw two fish. "Two more fish join them." Draw two more fish. "How many fish are in the water in all?" Point to each fish and count aloud, "1, 2, 3, 4. There are four fish in all."
3. Tell students another story problem and draw the fish. Repeat step 2 two more times with different combinations.

▲ Enrichment: Solving with Number Sentences

1. Give yourself and each student a dry-erase board and marker. Before the lesson, draw a number line from 1 to 10 at the top of your dry-erase board. Tell students that you are going to tell them a story problem and model how to write a number sentence to solve the problem.
2. Say, "Five fish are swimming in the water." Circle the number 5. "Three more fish join them." Draw arches from each number 5 to 8 as you count aloud, "1, 2, 3." Ask, "How many fish are in the water in all?" Write $5 + 3 = 8$. Show students how the number line helped you write the number sentence.
3. Tell students another story problem and have them write the number sentences on their papers. Repeat step 2 two more times with different combinations.

 Assess and Extend

Have students explain how to use numbers to help find out how many in all. Students should also explain the strategies they used.

Addition Word Problems

Color 5 apples green and 5 apples red. Cut out the apples. Use them to solve the problems.

1. There are 3 red apples and 4 green apples. How many apples are there in all? _____ apples	**2.** There are 5 red apples and 1 green apple. How many apples are there in all? _____ apples
3. There are 2 red apples and 3 green apples. How many apples are there in all? _____ apples	**4.** There are 2 red apples and 5 green apples. How many apples are there in all? _____ apples

cut

Addition Word Problems

Draw a picture to help you solve each problem.

1. There are 2 cats on the bed, and 4 more cats join them. How many cats are on the bed in all?

_____ cats

2. Sam has 4 trucks. His dad gives him 3 trucks. How many trucks does Sam have in all?

_____ trucks

3. Eboni put 3 stickers on a page. Sara puts on 2 more stickers. How many stickers are on the page now?

_____ pages

4. Bella has 2 rings. Her mom gives her 2 more rings. How many rings does Bella have now?

_____ rings

Addition Word Problems   ▲ Solving with Number Sentences

Write a number sentence to help you solve each problem.

1. Jose saw 5 birds. Abby saw 1 bird. How many birds did they see in all?

_____ + _____ = _____ birds

2. Kate has 3 fish. Drew has 4 fish. How many fish do they have in all?

_____ + _____ = _____ fish

3. Liam has 4 crackers. James has 4 crackers. How many crackers do they have in all?

_____ + _____ = _____ crackers

4. Grace kicked 2 balls. Finn kicked 6 balls. How many balls did they kick in all?

_____ + _____ = _____ balls

5. Zack ate 7 grapes. His brother ate 2 grapes. How many grapes did they eat in all?

_____ + _____ = _____ grapes

6. Heidi drew 6 pictures. Beth drew 3 pictures. How many pictures did they draw in all?

_____ + _____ = _____ pictures

Addition Story Problem Task Cards

David picked 5 apples. Sam picked 3 apples. How many apples did the boys pick in all?

A

Greg has 4 balloons. Lisa has 2 balloons. How many balloons do they have in all?

B

Paul has 5 toy trucks. James has 1 toy truck. How many trucks do they have in all?

C

Casey made 6 bracelets. Kira made 4 bracelets. How many bracelets did they make in all?

D

Amy washed 3 windows. Her sister washed 6 windows. How many windows did they wash in all?

E

Cole found 2 seashells. His mom found 8 seashells. How many seashells did they find in all?

F

Abby has 4 pets. Cindy has 5 pets. How many pets do they have in all?

G

Ella read 3 books. Felipe read 5 books. How many books did they read in all?

H

To prep: Copy on cardstock for durability. Cut apart the cards. Place them in a center with counters. If desired, include a recording sheet and pencils for students to mark with their answers.

Subtraction Word Problems

 Essential Question

How can objects and pictures be used to show a problem?

 Warm-Up/Review

Ask some students to come to the front of the room. Have the remaining students stay in their seats. Tell students that by bringing only some students up to the front, you were separating the large group into smaller groups. Remind students that when you separate groups of objects (or people in this case), you are subtracting.

 Mini-Lesson

Materials: sheets of green paper, red counters

1. Give each student a sheet of green paper and 10 red counters. Tell students that the green paper is a tree and the counters are apples.

2. Say, "There are 5 apples on a tree. Two apples fall out of the tree. How many apples are left on the tree?" Tell students that you are going to read the story again and model how to place the counters on the tree. Tell students to follow along with you and place their counters too. Say, "Five apples are on the tree." Place 5 red counters on the paper. "Two apples fall off of the tree." Move 2 counters off the paper. "How many apples are left on the tree?" Line up the counters that are on the paper and count aloud, "1, 2, 3. There are 3 apples left on the tree."

3. Tell students another story problem and place the counters on the paper. Repeat the story problem two more times with different combinations.

 Math Talk

How many objects did you start with?
How many objects did you take away from the first set?
How many objects do you have left?

 Journal Prompt

Have students explain how to use numbers to help find out how many are left. Students should also explain the strategies they used.

Materials

sheets of brown paper
orange counters
dry-erase boards
dry-erase markers

 Workstations

Activity sheets (pages 83–85)
Subtraction Story Problem Task
   Cards (page 86)

 Guided Math

⚪ **Remediation: Solving with Objects**

1. Give each student a sheet of brown paper and 10 orange counters. Tell students that the brown paper is a garden, and the counters are carrots.
2. Model how to use the counters to act out a story problem. Say, "There are 5 carrots planted in the garden." Place 5 orange counters on the paper. "The farmer picked 4 carrots." Move 4 counters off the paper. "How many carrots are left in the garden?" Line up the counters and count aloud, "One. There is 1 carrot in the garden."
3. Tell students another story problem and place the counters on the paper. Repeat step 2 two more times with different combinations.

◻ **On Level: Solving with Pictures**

1. Give yourself and each student a dry-erase board and marker. Tell students that you are going to tell them a story problem and show them how to draw pictures to solve the problem.
2. Say, "A farmer planted 7 carrots in the garden." Draw 7 carrots. "The farmer picked 3 carrots." Draw X's on three carrots. "How many carrots are left in the garden?" Point to each carrot and count aloud, "1, 2, 3, 4. There are 4 carrots left in the garden."
3. Tell students another story problem and draw the carrots. Repeat step 2 two more times with different combinations.

🔺 **Enrichment: Solving with Number Sentences**

1. Give yourself and each student a dry-erase board and marker. Before the lesson, draw a number line from 1 to 10 at the top of your dry-erase board. Tell students that you are going to tell them a story problem and model how to write a number sentence to solve the problem.
2. Say, "A farmer planted 9 carrots in the garden." Circle the number 9. Say, "The farmer picked 5 carrots." Draw arches from each number 9 to 4 as you count aloud, "1, 2, 3, 4, 5." Ask, "How many carrots are left in the garden?" Write 9 *take away 5 is 4* and 9 – 5 = 4. Show students how the number line helped you write the number sentence.
3. Tell students another story problem and have them write the number sentences on their papers. Repeat step 2 two more times with different combinations.

 Assess and Extend

Have each student draw a tree that has 7 apples on it. Have students draw X's on 4 apples that have fallen off their trees. Students should write the number that tells how many apples are left on their trees.

Subtraction Word Problems

⬤ Solving with Objects

Color and cut out the balloons. Use them to solve each problem.

1. You have 6 balloons. You pop 3 balloons. How many balloons do you have left?

_____ balloons

2. You have 8 balloons. You pop 2 balloons. How many balloons do you have left?

_____ balloons

3. You have 5 balloons. You pop 3 balloons. How many balloons do you have left?

_____ balloons

4. You have 7 balloons. You pop 1 balloon. How many balloons do you have left?

_____ balloons

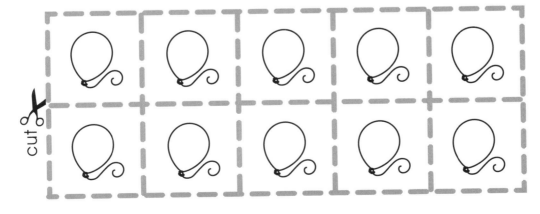

cut

Subtraction Word Problems   ☐ Solving with Pictures

Draw a picture to help you solve each problem.

1. There are 7 birds in the birdhouse. Three birds fly away. How many birds are left in the birdhouse? _____ birds	**2.** There are 5 butterflies on the bush. Four butterflies fly away. How many butterflies are left on the bush? _____ butterfly
3. There are 9 ants on the branch. Two ants fall off. How many ants are left on the branch? _____ ants	**4.** There are 8 ladybugs on the leaf. Five ladybugs fly away. How many ladybugs are left on the leaf? _____ ladybugs

Subtraction Word Problems ▲ Solving with Number Sentences

Write a number sentence to help you solve each problem.

1. Molly has 6 pieces of gum. She chews 1 piece of gum. How many pieces of gum does Molly have left?

_____ – _____ = _____ pieces

2. Ty has 8 coins. He loses 4 coins. How many coins does Ty have left?

_____ – _____ = _____ coins

3. Luke has 4 key chains. He gives away 1 key chain to a friend. How many key chains does Luke have left?

_____ – _____ = _____ key chains

4. Tara has 7 flowers. She gives 6 flowers to her grandma. How many flowers does Tara have left?

_____ – _____ = _____ flowers

5. Marla has 9 cherries. She eats 7 cherries. How many cherries does Marla have left?

_____ – _____ = _____ cherries

6. Henry has 5 cards. He gives 1 card to his brother. How many cards does Henry have left?

_____ – _____ = _____ cards

Subtraction Story Problem Task Cards

Mr. Ross bakes 5 pies. He sells 3 pies. How many pies does Mr. Ross have left?

A

Jesse has 6 pens. He gives a friend 2 pens. How many pens does Jesse have left?

B

Holly has 8 ice cubes in her cup. Two ice cubes melt. How many ice cubes are left in Holly's cup?

C

Cam has 7 baseballs. He hits 4 baseballs over a fence. How many baseballs does Cam have left?

D

Amy has 6 bracelets. She gives her sister 3 bracelets. How many bracelets does Amy have left?

E

Cole finds 8 seashells. He gives his mom 2 seashells. How many seashells does Cole have left?

F

The dog has 5 bones. He buries 2 bones. How many bones does he have left?

G

Lauren finds 7 beads. She gives 4 beads to her cousin. How many beads does Lauren have left?

H

To prep: Copy on cardstock for durability. Cut apart the task cards. Place the cards in a center with counters. If desired, include a recording sheet and pencils for students to mark with their answers.

Decomposing Numbers

Essential Question

How can the same number be shown in different ways?

Warm-Up/Review

Have students hold up 5 fingers. Most students will hold up one hand of 5 fingers. Ask students to hold up 5 fingers using both hands. Point out that there are many ways to show a number. Have students look around to see how other classmates show 5 fingers.

Mini-Lesson

Materials: linking cubes

1. Give each student 10 linking cubes. Have students count out 5 cubes as they link them together. Ask students to tell how many in all.

2. Next, model how to pick up the linked cubes by the ends (like holding an ear of corn). Ask students to "break" their linked cubes into two parts. Model how to write a number bond for the decomposition. Ask, "What number did we start with?" (5) Write 5 in the larger circle. Ask, "What numbers did we get when I broke the linked cubes?" (2 and 3) Write 2 and 3 in the two smaller circles. Tell students that this is a number bond. It shows how a large number can be broken into parts.

3. Have students relink their cubes and break the cube trains again. Have students share if they broke the 5 into different parts. Have a student share a different number bond for 5. (For example, 5 is 1 and 4.)

4. Challenge students to find the different parts for 6, 7, and 8.

5. Have students share what they notice about the numbers. Point out that the smaller numbers compose to the larger number, and the larger number decomposes to the smaller numbers.

Math Talk

Is there another way to show this number?
How many different ways are there to show this number?
If you know the parts, how do you know what the larger number is?

Journal Prompt

Explain how knowing all of the combinations for composing a number will help you in math.

Materials

two-color counters
two colors of linking cubes
dry-erase boards
dry-erase markers

 Workstations

Activity sheets (pages 89–91)
Rolling Number Bonds (page 92)

 Guided Math

⬤ **Remediation: Combinations to 5**

1. Give each student 5 two-color counters. Show students how to drop the counters onto the table. Line up the counters with red first and then yellow.
2. Have students drop their groups of 5 counters on the table and line them up. Tell students that each of them is showing 5, but in different ways. Have each student share how many red counters and yellow counters they have.
3. Challenge students to show all of the possible ways to make 5.

◻ **On Level: Combinations to 8**

1. Give each student 8 each of two colors of linking cubes. Show students how to make a linking cube train with 4 colored linking cubes. Then, add 4 more of a different color. Ask, "Is there another way to show 8 with two colors of linking cubes?"
2. Have students use their linking cubes to show 8 in any way they choose. Then, each student should lay her linking cube train on the table. Discuss the different combinations and what students notice about them.
3. Give each student a dry-erase board and marker. Challenge students to make a number bond for each way to show 8.

▲ **Enrichment: Combinations to 10**

1. Give each student 10 two-color counters. Show students how to drop the counters onto the table. Line up the counters with red first and then yellow.
2. Have students drop their groups of 10 counters on the table and line them up. Tell students that each of them is showing 10, but in different ways. Have students share how many red counters and yellow counters they have.
3. Give yourself and each student a dry-erase board and marker. On your dry-erase board, write *10 is 5 + 5*. Challenge students to list, on their dry-erase boards, all of the other possible ways to show 10 using addition statements. Discuss how *6 + 4* and *4 + 6* are both possibilities. (*commutative property*) Write students' addition statements on your dry-erase board.

 Assess and Extend

Have students list all of the combinations for the number 7. This number will be important as they use two dice to make sums. The number 7 comes up most often because it has the most combinations of all numbers from 2 to 12. (1 + 6, 6 + 1, 2 + 5, 5 + 2, 3 + 4, 4 + 3)

Decomposing Numbers   ● Combinations to 5

I. Color the circles to match the parts.

2 and 3

1 and 4

5 and 0

3 and 2

4 and 1

2. Write the missing number in each number bond.

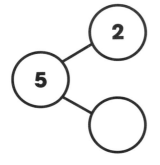 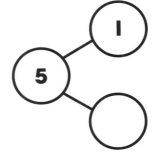 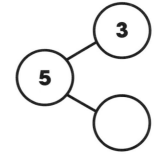

Decomposing Numbers

1. Color the circles to show the different ways to show 8. Write the numbers.

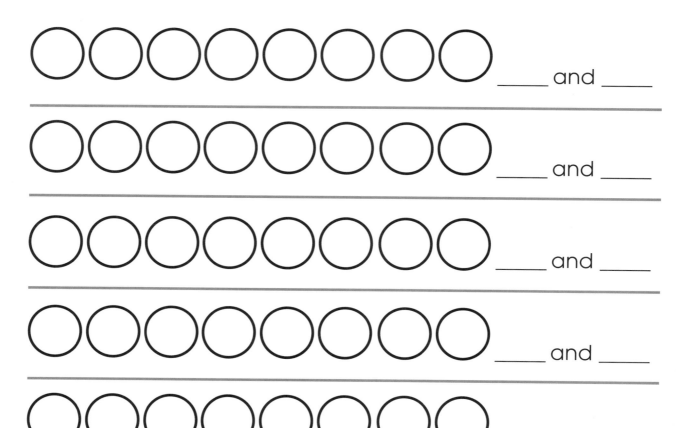

OOOOOOOO ____ and ____

OOOOOOOO ____ and ____

OOOOOOOO ____ and ____

OOOOOOOO ____ and ____

OOOOOOOO ____ and ____

2. Write the missing number in each number bond.

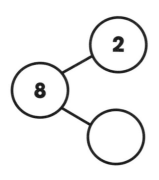 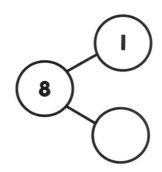 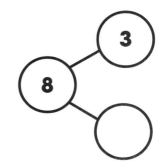

Decomposing Numbers   ▲ Combinations to 10

Write three ways to show each number using addition.

5 | _____ + _____ | | _____ + _____ | | _____ + _____ |

6 | _____ + _____ | | _____ + _____ | | _____ + _____ |

7 | _____ + _____ | | _____ + _____ | | _____ + _____ |

8 | _____ + _____ | | _____ + _____ | | _____ + _____ |

9 | _____ + _____ | | _____ + _____ | | _____ + _____ |

10 | _____ + _____ | | _____ + _____ | | _____ + _____ |

Rolling Number Bonds

Materials: number cubes (0–5)

Directions: Roll the dice. Write the numbers to complete the number bond.

Example: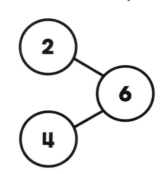

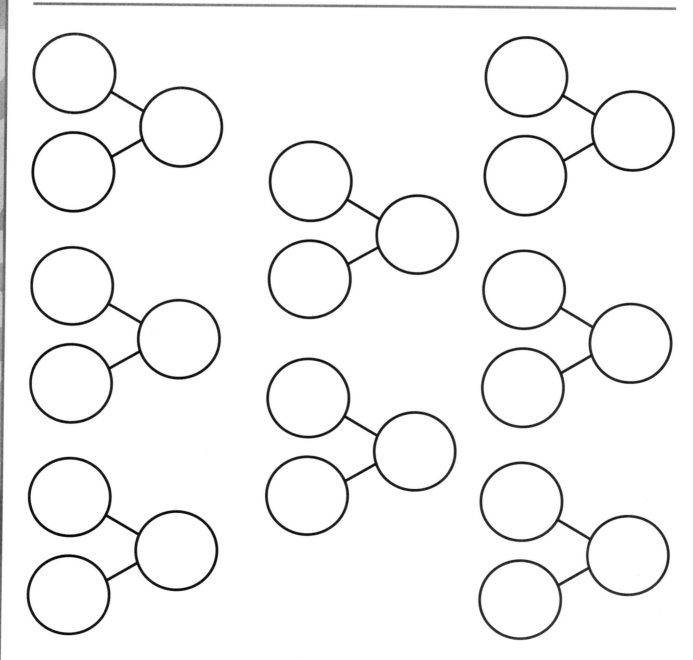

Making 10

 Essential Question

What are some different ways to make 10?

 Warm-Up/Review

Remind students that they have practiced finding different ways to make numbers. Have students hold up both hands and show 5 (6, 7, etc.).

 Mini-Lesson

Materials: chart paper, colored markers, two-color counters

1. Write the numbers 0 to 10 along the bottom of a sheet of chart paper. Tell students that they will help you make a rainbow for the combinations to 10.

2. Point to the *0*. Ask, "What number do we add to 0 to get 10?" (10) Use a red marker and draw a tall arch from 0 to 10. Point to the 1. Ask, "What number do we add to 1 to get 10?" (9) Use an orange marker to draw an arch from 1 to 9. Continue until you have drawn all of the arches.

3. Give each student 10 two-color counters. Have students line up the counters and flip them all to the red sides. Have students tell what combination to 10 this line represents. (0 and 10) Write it on the chart paper. Continue finding and recording all of the combinations to 10.

 Math Talk

What would we add to this number to make 10?

How many combinations for 10 can you make?

Which combination is the same, no matter what way the numbers are arranged?

 Journal Prompt

Explain why 4 + 6 and 6 + 4 are related addition sentences that both make 10.

Materials

counters
ten frames
sentence strips (see below)
dot stickers
business-sized envelopes (see below)
dry-erase boards and markers

 Workstations

Activity sheets (pages 95–97)
Roll to 10 (page 98)
Rolling Number Bonds (page 92)

 Guided Math

⦿ Remediation: Making 10 with Ten Frames

1. Give each student a set of 10 counters. Display a ten frame with 8 dots. Have students count aloud as you point to each dot. Ask, "How many more dots are needed to make 10?" Model how to say the answer. Say, "I have 8 dots. I need 2 more dots to make 10." Continue with a few more examples.
2. Give each student a ten frame and two-color counters. Tell students a number 0 to 10 and have them place the counters on their ten frames. Then, ask students to find how many more to make 10 using another color of counter. Continue with a few more examples.

▢ On Level: Making 10 with Number Bonds

1. Before the lesson, make a set of sentence strips with 10 dot stickers in a row on each. Cut the short ends off a set of business-sized envelopes.
2. Tell students that you have a strip with 10 dots. Slide the strip inside an envelope so that four dots are hidden. Have students count aloud as you point to the number of dots showing. (6) Ask students to tell how many dots are hiding. (4)
3. Tell students that you can write a number bond using the numbers they do know. On a dry-erase board, show students how to write 10 in the left circle and 6 in another circle. Then, have students find the missing number and fill in the blank circle.
4. Give pairs of students a strip, envelope, dry-erase board, and dry-erase marker. Challenge one student to hide part of a 10 and have the other student write the number bond. Have them switch and repeat the activity.

▲ Enrichment: Making 10 with Number Sentences

1. Before the lesson, make a set of sentence strips with 10 dot stickers in a row on each. Cut the short ends off a set of business-sized envelopes.
2. Tell students that you have a strip with 10 dots. Slide the strip inside an envelope so that four dots are hidden. Have students count aloud as you point to the number of dots showing. (6) Ask students to tell how many dots are hiding. (4)
3. Tell students that you can write a number sentence for the numbers you do know. On a dry-erase board, write *10 is 6 and __* and *10 = 6 + __*. Ask students to find the missing numbers using what they know about combinations to 10. Fill in the missing numbers in the number sentences.
4. Give pairs of students a strip, envelope, dry-erase board, and dry-erase marker. Challenge one student to hide part of a 10 and have the other student write the number sentence. Have them switch and repeat the activity.

 Assess and Extend

Have students find combinations to make 10. Write the numbers 0 to 10. Have students use crayons to draw the rainbow arches to show combinations to 10.

Making 10 ● Making 10 with Ten Frames

Draw the missing dots. Write the number to make 10.

1. 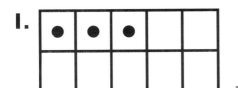 _____

2. 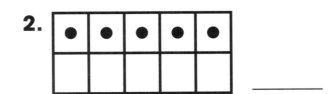 _____

3. 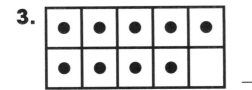 _____

4. 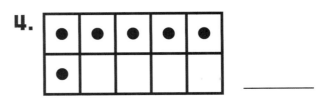 _____

5. 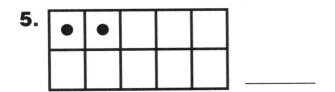 _____

6. 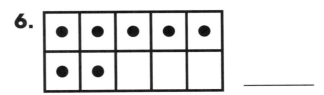 _____

7. 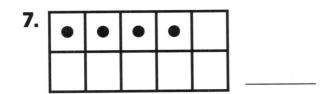 _____

8. 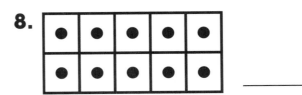 _____

9. 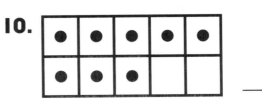 _____

10. 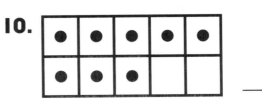 _____

Making 10

Write the missing number in each number bond. Color the circles to show the sets.

1.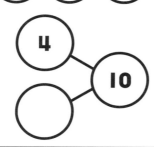

2.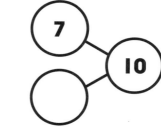

3.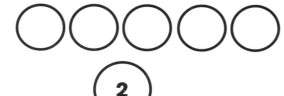

4.

5.

6.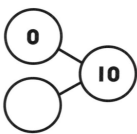

Making 10

Color the boxes to show different ways to make 10.
Complete the number sentences.

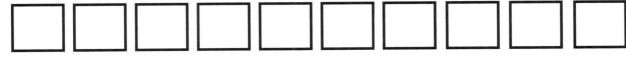

_____ + _____ = 10

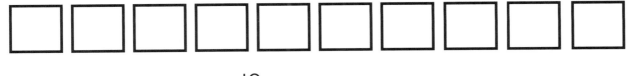

_____ + _____ = 10

_____ + _____ = 10

_____ + _____ = 10

_____ + _____ = 10

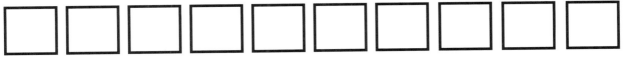

_____ + _____ = 10

Roll to 10

Materials: number cube (0–5), two colors of crayons

To play: Each player chooses a color of crayon. Players take turns. Roll the number cube. Color the number that, when added to the number on the cube, makes 10. If you cannot color a number, play passes to the next player. The player with the most squares colored wins.

10	6	8	5
7	9	7	8
9	5	8	10
6	10	9	7
7	8	7	6
9	6	10	8

Patterning

 Warm-Up/Review

Have students look for things around the classroom that have stripes, dots, or other patterns. Challenge students to describe a pattern; if it repeats, students should be able to tell how. For example, *Dan's shirt has stripes. The pattern is blue stripe, red stripe, blue stripe, red stripe.*

 Mini-Lesson

Materials: linking cubes

1. Clap a pattern such as *clap-clap pause clap-clap pause.* Have students repeat it. Do this several times with various pattern units. Add foot stomps, lap taps, or other movements to the pattern.

2. Tell students that they just made a *pattern.* The pattern repeats.

3. Tell students that they can *extend* the pattern by continuing to repeat the pattern for a longer time. Have students stand in a circle. Explain that you are going to act out a pattern. Keep the pattern simple such as, *clap-stomp pause.* Then, one by one, have each student (in order) repeat the pattern. Extend the pattern around the circle.

4. Tell students that they will make a pattern with linking cubes. Show students a row of linking cubes in this pattern: red, blue, red, blue, red, blue. Tell students that this pattern is the same as *clap-stomp.* There are two items repeated. We can name the pattern *AB* because *A* (clap/red) and *B* (stomp/blue) is the part that is being repeated.

5. Give each student two colors of linking cubes and ask them to make the same pattern. Have each student compare the pattern with a neighbor and practice reading the pattern by color and by letter.

6. Challenge students to use the cubes to make *AAB* or *ABB* patterns.

 Math Talk

How do you know that this is a pattern?
What can you do to this pattern to
    change it?
How can you extend this pattern?

 Journal Prompt

Explain how you know that something is a pattern.

Materials

linking cubes
pattern blocks
dry-erase boards
dry-erase markers

 Workstations

Activity sheets (pages 101–103)
Pattern Play (page 104)

 Guided Math

⬤ Remediation: Naming Patterns

1. Before the lesson, create one linking cube pattern for each student in the group and one for you. Be sure that each pattern is different in some way (*AB, ABC, AAB, ABB*, etc.). Place extra, unattached cubes in the center of the table.
2. Use your cube set to model how to name, describe, and extend the pattern. Say, "I see 2 colors that repeat: red, blue, red, blue. I can also describe the pattern as *AB, AB*." Write the name of the pattern on the board. Then, say, "I can use the pattern to determine what comes next: *red, blue*." Write the name of the pattern on the board.
3. Have students describe their patterns. Challenge students to name their patterns using letters. Switch sets and repeat.

▪ On Level: Extending Patterns

1. Use pattern blocks to create a simple AB repeating pattern. Model how to describe the pattern by color, shape, or pattern unit (for example, AB, AB, AB), as well as how to extend the pattern.
2. Have students create their own patterns using the blocks (for example, AB, ABC, AAB, or ABB) and "read" their patterns by color, shape, or pattern unit.
3. Pair students. In each pair, have one partner create a pattern with the pattern blocks and then challenge his partner to extend the pattern with more pattern blocks. Have them switch roles and repeat.

▲ Enrichment: Translating Patterns

1. Use pattern blocks to create an ABB repeating pattern. Ask, "What is the repeated unit in this pattern? How do we name the pattern using letters?" Write the name of the pattern on the board.
2. Tell students that you would like them to make an ABB pattern as well. However, they need to use different pattern blocks than you just used. Have students make the ABB pattern. Explain to students that they have translated your pattern, which is to make a pattern that matches an original pattern but with different objects or attributes. Tell students that the second pattern will have the same pattern name. In this case, it is also ABB.
3. Give each student a dry-erase board and marker. Have students draw a more complex shape pattern (for example, AABC, ABCB, ABBB, or ABBAC) on their dry-erase boards. Then, have each student switch boards with another group member. Each student should draw a new translated pattern below the original pattern.

 Assess and Extend

Have each student draw a pattern, circle the repeating unit of the pattern, and name the pattern. Challenge students to translate their patterns by using different shapes, objects, etc.

Patterning

Color and name each pattern.

Example:

ABB _____

1.  _____

2.  _____

3.  _____

4.  _____

Draw an AB pattern.

✚➖ Patterning
✖️➗

● Naming Patterns

Extend each pattern.

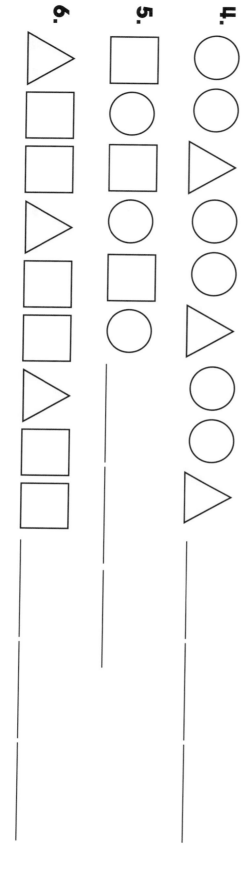

1.

2.

3.

4.

5.

6.

Patterning

Copy each pattern using shapes.

1.

2.

3.

4.

Pattern Play

Materials: manipulatives (pattern blocks, linking cubes, counters, etc.)

Directions: Choose a pattern name card. Use the objects to make a matching pattern.

AB	**AAB**
ABB	**ABA**
ABC	**ABCD**
AABB	**ABBA**
ABCC	**AABC**
ABBC	**AABC**

To prep: Copy on card stock and laminate for durability. Cut out the pattern name cards. Place the cards in a center with the materials and directions.

Essential Question

How can 1 ten and some ones be added to make the numbers 11 to 19?

Warm-Up/Review

Have students count aloud to 10 while doing jumping jacks. Then, have students count from 11 to 20 while hopping in place. Finally, have students count from 1 to 20 while doing jumping jacks. They should switch to hopping in place when they get to 10.

⭐ Mini-Lesson

Materials: ten frames, counters

1. Give each student 19 counters and a ten frame. Tell students to fill in their ten frames. Ask, "Will all of the counters fit in the ten frame? Why not?" (No, a ten frame only has space for 10 counters.) Tell students to move the extra counters to the side. Tell students that they have 10 and some more counters. Say, "Let's explore how to show numbers 11 to 19 using double ten frames." Give each student another ten frame.

2. Display a number, such as 13. Have students place 10 counters on the first ten frame. Have students place the counters that did not fit on the first ten frame on the second ten frame. Tell students that 13 is a group of ten and three more.

3. Have students explore the numbers 11, 15, and 18 with the counters and ten frames.

Math Talk

Is this number more than 10? How do you know?

Will this number of counters fit on one ten frame? Two ten frames? How do you know?

Can you think of another way to show this number?

Journal Prompt

Draw a double ten frame. Show the number 16 on the frame.

Materials

yarn circles (see below)
counters
ten frames
number cards 11–19

 Workstations

Activity sheets (pages 107–109)
Ten and Some More Match
(page 110)

 Guided Math

⚪ Remediation: Ten and Some More

1. Before the lesson, tie 12-inch lengths of yarn into circles, making enough to give one to each student. Give each student 19 counters and one circle of yarn.
2. Display a number, such as 14. Have students show 14 with their counters. Encourage students to organize the counters in neat rows to make counting easier.
3. Model for students how to identify a group of 10 counters and place the string around the group. Say, "Ten counters are inside the circle. Some counters are outside the circle. Let's count how many are outside the circle. 1, 2, 3, 4. 10 and 4 more is 14."
4. Give each student a ten frame. Have students move their counters onto the ten frames. Ask, "Do I have enough counters to fill the ten frame? Why or why not?" Explain that just like in their yarn circles, the ten frames each hold 10 counters. Have students count the counters that do not fit in their ten frames to confirm that it is still 4.
5. Challenge students to show the numbers 12 and 15, first by "circling" a group of ten with the yarn and then by using a ten frame.

⬜ On Level: Using a Double Ten Frame

1. Give each student 19 counters and a double ten frame. Display a number, such as 14. Have students show 14 with their counters. Tell students that they must fill the first ten frame completely before placing counters in the next ten frame.
2. Ask, "Do I have enough counters to fill the ten frame? Why or why not?" Explain that the ten frames each hold 10 counters. Have students count the counters that do not fit in their first ten frames to confirm that it is 4. Say, "We know it is 14 because one full ten frame holds 10. We can count on from 10: 11, 12, 13, 14." Ask students to share another reason why it is 14.
3. Challenge students to show the numbers 16 and 18 in the double ten frame and to count on from 10 each time.

▲ Enrichment: Writing Number Sentences

1. Give each student 19 counters and a double ten frame. Display a number, such as 17. Have students show 17 with their counters. Tell students that they must fill the first ten frame completely before placing counters in the next ten frame.
2. Tell students that because we know the first ten frame is 10, they can write addition number sentences for what the frame shows. Model how to write a number sentence for 17. *10 and 7 is 17*, and *10 + 7 = 17.*
3. Challenge students to show the numbers 16 and 18 in the double ten frame and write number sentences for each.

 Assess and Extend

Have students explain how the number 15 is composed of a ten and some ones. Ask, "What would that look like on a double ten frame? As a number sentence? To make 16, how many more counters would I need to place in the second ten frame?"

Tens and Ones

⬤ Ten and Some More

Circle each group of 10. Write the number of ones. Write the total.

1.

10 and _____ is _____ .

2.

10 and _____ is _____ .

3.

10 and _____ is _____ .

4.

10 and _____ is _____ .

5.

10 and _____ is _____ .

Tens and Ones

Fill in the ten frames. Write the missing numbers.

1. 12

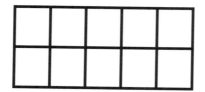 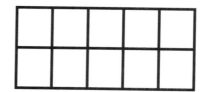

10 and _____ is 12.

2. 15

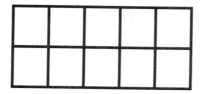 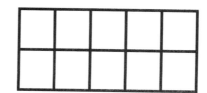

10 and _____ is 15.

3. 11

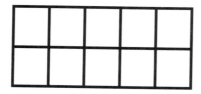 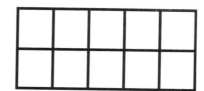

10 and _____ is 11.

4. 14

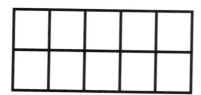 

10 and _____ is 14.

5. 17

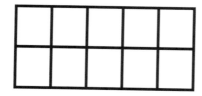 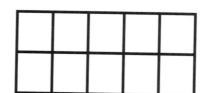

10 and _____ is 17.

Tens and Ones ▲ Writing Number Sentences

Write each number. Write the numbers to complete the number sentence.

1. 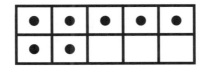 _____

10 + _____ = _____

2. 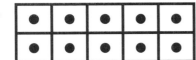 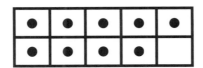 _____

10 + _____ = _____

3. 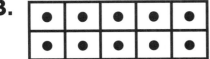 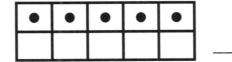 _____

10 + _____ = _____

4. 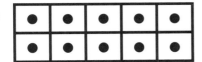 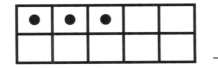 _____

10 + _____ = _____

Ten and Some More Match

To play: Player 1 puts all of the cards facedown. He turns over one long card and one short card. If the cards show the same amount, the player keeps the pair. If the cards do not show the same amount, the player puts the cards facedown, and play passes to the next player. The player with the most pairs at the end wins.

		11
		12
		13
		14
		15
		16
		17
		18
		19

To prep: Copy on card stock and laminate for durability. Cut apart the cards. Place them in a center with the directions.

Essential Question

How can the numbers 11 to 19 be separated into 1 ten and some ones?

Warm-Up/Review

Hold up double ten frames that show various numbers of dots from 11 to 19. Have students say aloud the number that each double ten frame shows.

 Mini-Lesson

Materials: base ten blocks, number bond mats, number cards 11–19

1. Display the number 10 and a filled ten frame. Ask students to raise their hands if they agree that these numbers are the same. Tell students that you are going to show them another way to show 10. Tell students that a tower of 10 cubes is called a ten. Hold up the base ten block tens rod. Tell students that because 10 little cubes make a tens rod, it is called a *ten*.

2. Give each student a number bond mat, number cards 11 to 19, and base ten blocks. Display the number 14. Ask, "How many tens are in 14?" Have students place their number 14 cards on the mat in the "whole" circle. Then, model how 14 is made up of 1 ten and 4 ones by placing a tens rod in one of the "part" circles and 4 cubes in the other "part" circle. Have students do the same. Say, "14 is 10 and 4."

3. Have students explore the concept with at least two more numbers.

 Math Talk

How do we know that this number has 1 ten?
Which number is 10 and this many ones?
How many rods and cubes do you need to show this number?

 Journal Prompt

Explain how to break a number 11 to 19 into a ten and ones.

Materials

laminated number bond mats
linking cubes
dry-erase markers
base ten blocks
number cards 11–19

 Workstations

Activity sheets (pages 113–115)
Tens and Ones Number Puzzles
(page 116)
Ten and Some More Match
(page 110)

 Guided Math

⚪ **Remediation: Decomposing Numbers**

1. Give each student a number bond mat and 19 linking cubes. Display the number 11. Have students write *11* on the mat in the "whole" circle and place 11 linking cubes on top.
2. Tell students that they are going to separate the number into parts. One part will be ten, and the other part will be one. Have students link 10 cubes together and put the linked cubes into one of the part circles. Then, have students place the remaining linking cube in the other part circle. Have students say aloud with you, "11 is 10 and 1," as you point to each part of the number bond mat.
3. Repeat with the numbers 13 and 15.

🔲 **On Level: Using Base Ten Blocks**

1. Give each student 19 base ten blocks and a set of number cards 11 to 19.
2. Model how to show a number using base ten blocks. Display the number *17*. Talk through choosing a tens rod and 7 ones cubes.
3. Have each student choose a card and use the base ten blocks to show the number. Remind students that the numbers 11 to 19 are composed of a ten and some ones, so therefore, each of them should start with a tens rod when showing the number. Help students as needed.
4. Have students choose and show 3 more numbers to a partner.

🔺 **Enrichment: Writing Number Sentences**

1. Give each student 19 base ten blocks and a set of number cards 11 to 19.
2. Model how to show a number using base ten blocks and write a number sentence. Display the number *16*. Choose a tens rod and 6 ones cubes. Write *16 is 10 and 6*, and *16 = 10 + 6*.
3. Have each student choose a card and use the base ten blocks to show the number. Then, have each student write a number sentence to match.
4. Have students choose three more numbers and write a number sentence for each.

 Assess and Extend

Have students choose a number 11 to 19. Then, have students write the number bond. Students should use pictures, blocks, or numbers to show the parts.

Decomposing Numbers 11–19   ● Decomposing Numbers

Complete the number bonds.

1.
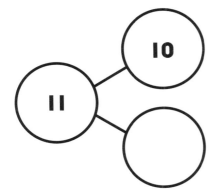

2.
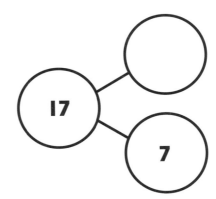

3.
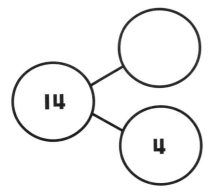

4.
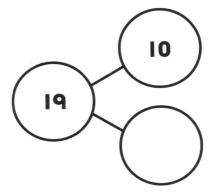

5.
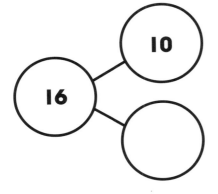

6.
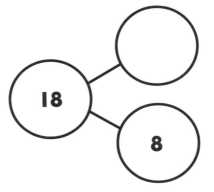

Decomposing Numbers 11–19 ☐ Using Base Ten Blocks

Say each number. Color the blocks to show the number.

1. 13

2. 16

3. 17

4. 14

5. 18

6. 12

Decomposing Numbers 11–19   ▲ Writing Number Sentences

Look at the base ten blocks. Write the numbers and number sentences.

1.

_____ = _____ + _____

2.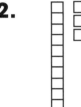

_____ = _____ + _____

3.

_____ = _____ + _____

4.

_____ = _____ + _____

5.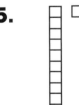

_____ = _____ + _____

6.

_____ = _____ + _____

Tens and Ones Number Puzzles

Directions: Choose a bag. Join the matching pieces.

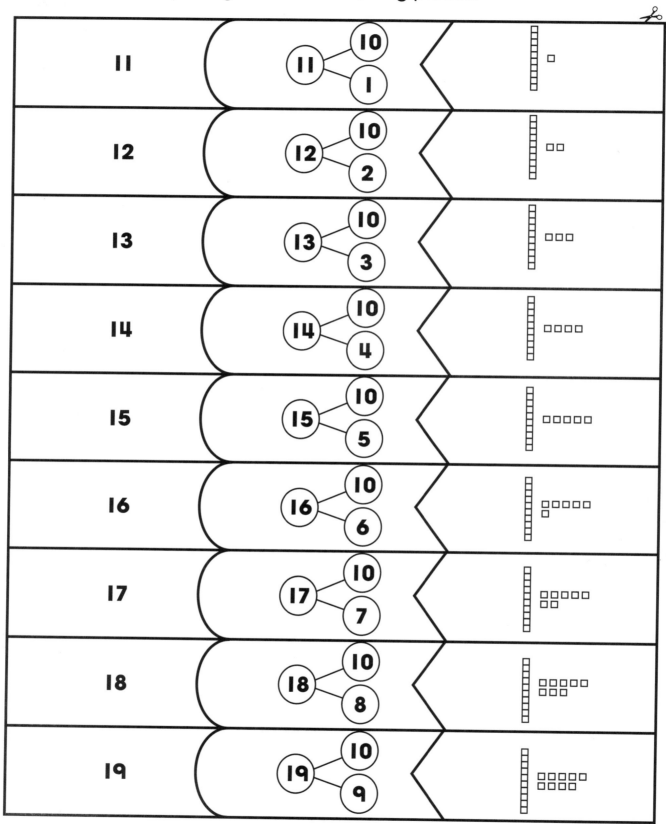

Essential Question

What are some ways to describe length and weight?

 ## Warm-Up/Review

Have students think about and share times that we measure things. Tell students to think about when they go to the doctor. Nurses record their weight and height. Have students share other things that we might weigh or whose length we would measure.

 ## Mini-Lesson

Materials: classroom objects (see below)

1. Before the lesson, gather some short, long, light, and heavy objects. Display them at the front of the classroom.

2. Have a student come to the front of the classroom and choose an object. Tell her to describe it. Guide her to describe how it looks and feels. As the student describes the object, write the describing words that she uses. Ask several more students to come to the front of the classroom, choose objects, and describe them. Write the words that they use.

3. Tell students that many words can be used to describe the objects. Today, you want them to focus on the words that describe an object's size. Have students notice any words on the board that describe size (for example, large, small, long, heavy, etc.).

4. Circle the words and add any others that are missing or that the students think of. Tell students that size can be measured. Remind them of the nurses measuring height and weight.

5. Pair students to have them play a game of I Spy. Encourage students to use measurement words to describe the objects.

 ## Math Talk

Can you find an object you think is heavy? Light?

Can you find an object you think is short? Long/tall?

Is it possible to have two heavy objects? Tall objects? How can you describe them both?

 ## Journal Prompt

Explain how an object can be long and light.

Materials

preprogrammed sticky notes
(see below)
preprogrammed index cards
(see below)
linking cubes

 Workstations

Activity sheets (pages 119–121)
Measurement Sorting Mats
(page 122)

 Guided Math

⭕ Remediation: Assigning Attributes

1. Before the lesson, program sticky notes with the words *short, tall, light,* and *heavy*. Make enough for each student to have one of each.
2. Give each student one of each sticky note. Tell students to walk around the classroom and place their sticky notes on objects they think the words describe.
3. Have students return to the group. Ask, "What did you notice? How did you decide which objects to put the notes on?"
4. Pair students and challenge them to draw or make lists of short objects, tall objects, light objects, and heavy objects. Allow pairs to share their ideas.

⬜ On Level: Identifying Measurable Attributes

1. Before the lesson, program index cards with the words *short, tall, light* and *heavy*. Also include other descriptors such as color, texture, etc. Display four objects that could be described as short, tall, light, and heavy.
2. Have students look at and feel each object. Read the index cards and place them on the table. Ask students to assign the words to the objects. Tell students that some of these words describe size and can be measured. Have students remove the words that cannot be measured.
3. Challenge students to draw pictures of objects that can also be described as short, tall, light, and heavy.

🔺 Enrichment: Comparing Measurable Attributes

1. Give each student a different number of linking cubes. Have students link their cubes. Then, have students decide if their linked cube "towers" are short or tall. Ask, "Who has the tallest? Shortest? How do you know?"
2. Have students line up their towers next to other students' towers and make decisions about which ones are short and which ones are tall. Say, "Your tower might be short when you compare it to your neighbor's, but tall when you compare it to mine." (Display a tower of two cubes.) Explain that to be able to say that something is short, tall, light, or heavy, you often need to have something to compare it to.
3. Challenge students to list or draw pairs of objects that can be described as short and tall, and light and heavy.

 Assess and Extend

Have each student draw the following: an object that is heavy, an object that is light, an object that is short, and an object that is long or tall.

Measurable Attributes ● Assigning Attributes

Draw a picture of something you can describe with each word.

light	heavy
short	**tall/long**

Measurable Attributes   ☐ Identifying Measurable Attributes

Circle the word that best describes each object.

1.

light   heavy

2.

light   heavy

3.

light   heavy

4.

light   heavy

5.

short   tall

6.

short   tall

7.

short   tall

8.

short   tall

Measurable Attributes   ▲ Comparing Measurable Attributes

Complete each sentence. Draw a picture.

I am lighter than _____ _____ .	I am heavier than _____ _____ .
I am shorter than _____ _____ .	I am taller than _____ _____ .

Measurement Sorting Mats

Materials: sorting mat, cards

Directions: Choose a mat. Put two header cards on the sorting mat. Lay out the picture cards. Sort them on the mat.

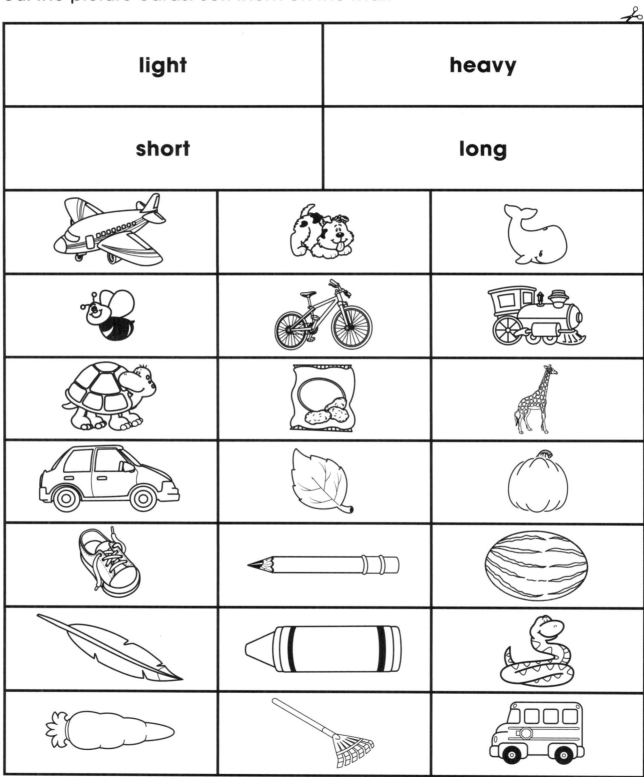

light	heavy
short	long

Comparing Objects

Essential Question

How can two objects be compared?

Warm-Up/Review

Have students recall in the previous lesson how they used specific words to compare objects. These words had to do with length and weight. Have students help you make an anchor chart for the comparative words. Have students share words as you list them on the chart. Be sure to include the words *length, shorter, longer, taller, weight, lighter,* and *heavier.*

Mini-Lesson

Materials: classroom objects

1. Ask students to choose one object each from the classroom and bring the objects to the rug.

2. Choose one student to stand and show an object. Ask, "Who has something shorter than this (object)?" Compare the two objects and have the newest volunteer explain why her object is shorter.

3. Instruct the first student to sit and the second to remain standing. Ask, "Who has something longer than this (object)?" Compare the two objects and have the newest volunteer explain why his object is longer.

4. Repeat this process several times to reinforce the concepts of shorter and longer.

5. Follow the same steps to explain the concepts of weight, lighter, and heavier.

Math Talk

Will the shorter object always be lighter? Explain.

Will the longer object always be heavier? Explain.

How can an object be described as heavy one time and light the next? Explain.

Journal Prompt

Explain why one student might say a book is heavy, and another student might say the book is light.

Materials

classroom objects (see below)
paper clips (large and small)
pan balance

 Workstations

Activity sheets (pages 125–127)
Grab and Color (page 128)
Measurement Sorting Mats
(page 122)

 Guided Math

⬤ **Remediation: Describing Weight and Length**
1. Gather short, long, light, and heavy objects to compare (for example, pencils, envelopes, small but heavy rocks, long but light paperback books, short but heavy hardcover chapter books, etc.).
2. Choose two objects and place them on the table. Model how to describe their length and weight using comparative words. Say, for example, "The paperback book is longer than the hardcover book, but the hardcover book is heavier."
3. Challenge each student to compare objects. Encourage use of the words *length, shorter, longer, weight, lighter,* and *heavier.*

◼ **On Level: Comparing and Ordering Objects**
1. Gather short, long, light, and heavy objects to compare (see examples above).
2. Have each student place any three objects in order from lightest to heaviest and then talk about the objects' weights using comparative words.
3. Repeat step 2, this time placing the same objects in order from shortest to longest. Discuss the objects' lengths using comparative words.
4. Challenge each student to compare three objects. Encourage use of the words *length, shorter, shortest, longer, longest, weight, lighter, lightest, heavier,* and *heaviest.*

▲ **Enrichment: Measuring with Nonstandard Units**
1. Gather objects to compare (see above).
2. Have students place three objects in order from lightest to heaviest and then talk about the objects' weights using comparative words. Repeat by having them place the objects in order from shortest to longest.
3. Place small and large paper clips and a pan balance on the table. Have students find the length of each object in nonstandard units, first using small paper clips and then using large paper clips. Have them record their results (for example, *pencil = 12 small paper clips*). Have students repeat with weight using the pan balance.
4. Have students share their results. Challenge students by asking, "How did the measurements change when using different-sized paper clips? Why do you think the measurements changed?"

 Assess and Extend

Show students three objects. Have students order the objects by length and use comparative words to describe their reasoning for the order.

Comparing Objects   ● Describing Weight and Length

Circle the object in each pair that is lighter.

1.      **2.**

Circle the object in each pair that is heavier.

3.         **4.**

Circle the object in each pair that is shorter.

5.

6.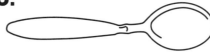

Circle the object in each pair that is longer.

7.

8.

Comparing Objects ▢ Comparing and Ordering Objects

I. Number each set of objects in order from 1 (lightest) to 3 (heaviest).

_____   _____   _____

_____   _____   _____

2. Number the boxes in order from 1 (shortest) to 3 (longest).

 _____

 _____

 _____

3 inch pencil _____

1 inch pencil _____

5 inch pencil _____

Name _____   Date _____

Measure the length of each box. Use small and large paper clips.

1.

About _____ small paper clips long

About _____ large paper clips long

2.

About _____ small paper clips long

About _____ large paper clips long

3.

About _____ small paper clips long

About _____ large paper clips long

4. Draw your pencil. Measure the length of your pencil with small and large paper clips.

About _____ small paper clips long

About _____ large paper clips long

Grab and Color

Materials: bag of at least 16 objects (pencils, markers, highlighters, colored pencils, pens, etc.), two colors of crayons

To play: Each player chooses a color of crayon. Players take turns reaching into the bag and pulling out an object. Players compare the objects. The player with the longer or heavier object colors a square on his caterpillar. The first player to color his whole caterpillar wins.

Round 1—What's Longer?

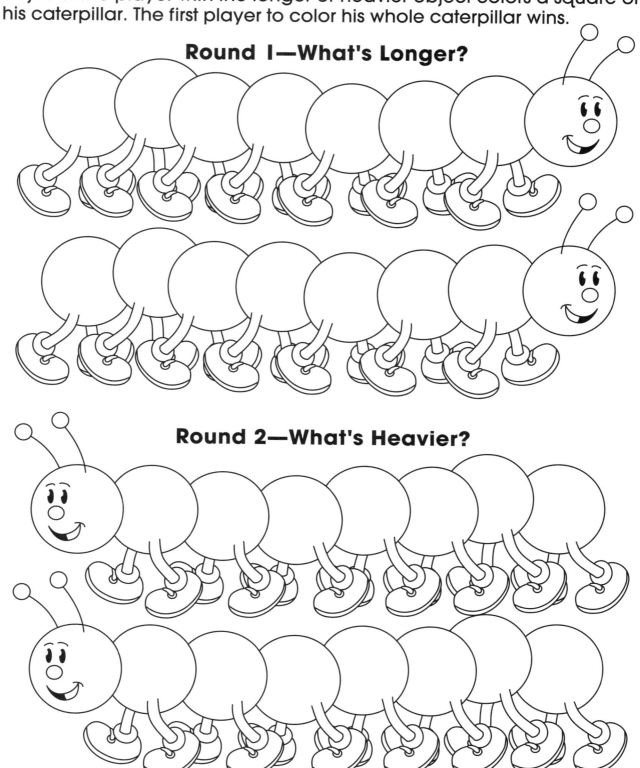

Round 2—What's Heavier?

Essential Question

How can objects be sorted and classified?

 Warm-Up/Review

Have students come to the rug for the group lesson, calling them by certain attributes. Say, for example, "Anyone wearing sneakers, please come to the rug." Tell students that you are using attributes (in this case, types of clothing they are wearing) to call them to the rug.

 Mini-Lesson

Materials: three different colored sheets of paper

1. Before the lesson, hang a sheet of each color of paper: blue, red, and yellow (or another set of three colors) on a classroom wall. Tell students to look at each color, decide which they like best, and then stand by the color.

2. Tell students that they classified themselves by the colors that they liked best. Next, tell them that you want them to look at what they are wearing today, decide which color they are wearing the most of, and stand by that color. If some students do not have any of the colors on their clothing, have them sit on the rug. Tell students that now they have classified themselves by the color of their clothing.

3. Have students join the other students on the rug. Tell them that the number of students was the same each time. What changed is how they were sorted. Review the words *classify* and *sort*.

4. Tell students to remove one shoe each and place it in the center of the circle. Once students have placed all shoes in the circle, have students share ideas for how they could sort the shoes (for example, laces/no laces, boots/sneakers/sandals, etc.). Try each sort.

 Math Talk

Which color did you move to and why?
Was the second color you chose different from the first? Why or why not?
Did the number of students stay the same or change? Explain.

 Journal Prompt

Explain how you might use sorting at a grocery store.

Materials

linking cubes
attribute blocks

 Workstations

Activity sheets (pages 131–133)
Button Sort (page 134)

 Guided Math

⬤ Remediation: Sorting by One Attribute

1. Give each student a set of linking cubes that contains only two different colors of cubes.
2. Ask students to tell what is different about the cubes in their sets. (They are different colors.) Have students sort the cubes into piles by color. Have students link the cubes in each pile.
3. Have students count the number of each color of cubes and share their counts. Then, ask, "How many more of one color do you have than the other color?" Model for students how to place the linked cube towers next to each other and break off the extra piece to make sure the towers are even. Then, break apart the extra piece and count the cubes.

▢ On Level: Sorting by Two Attributes

1. Give each student a set of same-sized attribute blocks that contains only two different colors and two different shapes (for example, blue and red squares and triangles).
2. Ask students to tell what they notice about the blocks in their sets. (They are different colors. They are different shapes.) Have students sort the blocks into piles by color. Have students count each pile and tell which has more and less.
3. Have each student put his blocks back into a pile. Have students sort the blocks again, this time by shape. Have students count each pile and tell which has more and less.
4. Pair students and challenge them to switch sets and sort the blocks. Ask students to share the attributes they sorted by and tell which groups have more and less.

▲ Enrichment: Sorting, Classifying, and Graphing Data

1. Give each student a set of attribute blocks that contains three different shapes.
2. Ask students to share what shapes they have in their sets. Have students sort the blocks into piles by shape. Tell students that they classified the blocks by telling what shape each one is. Then, they sorted the blocks by shape into three piles, or categories.
3. Have students line up each pile to make it easier for them to compare the amount of shapes per pile. Encourage students to match the shapes one to one in columns. Tell students that by lining up the shapes, they have created a graph. Explain how a graph makes it easier to answer questions about the objects being sorted without having to count. Have students compare each column and tell which has more, less, and the same amount.
4. Pair students and challenge them to switch sets and then sort and graph the blocks.

 Assess and Extend

Show students a set of attribute blocks that have three colors and three shapes. Ask students to tell how many ways they could sort the blocks.

Classifying and Sorting Objects   Sorting by One Attribute

Cut out the pictures. Sort and glue the pictures. Then, write how many.

fish	bird	frog

How many ? _____

How many ? _____

How many ? _____

cut

Classifying and Sorting Objects ☐ Sorting by Two Attributes

Cut out the pictures. Sort and glue the pictures. Then, write how many.

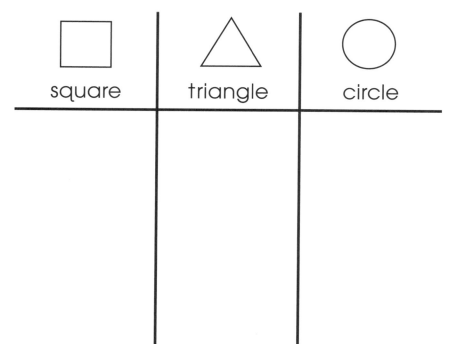

□	△	○
square	triangle	circle

How many □ ? _____

How many △ ? _____

How many ○ ? _____

How many small shapes? _____

How many large shapes? _____

✂ cut □ ○ △ □ ○ △

Classifying and Sorting Objects ▲ Sorting, Classifying, and Graphing Data

Cut out the shapes. Sort and glue the shapes in the graph. Then, write how many.

Number of Shapes

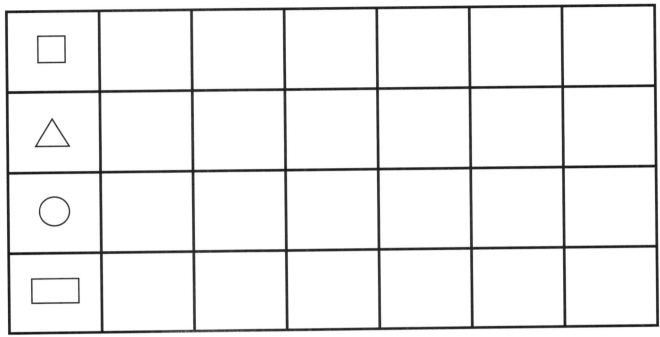

How many ☐ ? _____   How many △ ? _____

How many ○ ? _____   How many ▭ ? _____

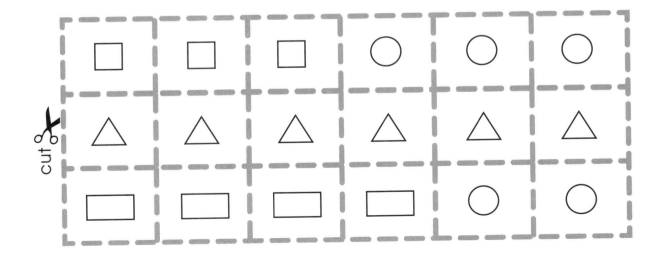

Button Sort

Materials: buttons, sorting mats

Directions: Choose a sorting mat. Sort the buttons on the mat.

big	small
2 holes	**4 holes**
round	**square**
smooth	**bumpy**
plastic	**wooden**

To prep: Copy on card stock for durability. Glue each header to a side of an open file folder to create five sorting mats. Place the mats in a center with the materials and directions.

Essential Question

How can data be shown on a graph?

 Warm-Up/Review

Ask students to raise their hands to answer the questions. Then ask, "Who has a brother? Who has a sister? Who has a cat? Who has a dog?" Count the number of raised hands each time. Tell students that you are collecting data.

 Mini-Lesson

Materials: bags, masking tape (optional)

1. Before the lesson, list 3 to 4 objects commonly found outside the school (for example, twig, small rock, leaf, and pinecone). Make one copy of the list for every 2 to 3 students.

2. Take the class outside for a short nature scavenger hunt. Divide students into groups of 2 or 3. Give each group a bag and the list of objects to find.

3. Have students search for as many of each object as they can find and put them into their bags, allowing only three minutes for students to do so.

4. Return to the classroom. Have students work together to sort the collected objects on the floor or the table and arrange the objects in columns, similar to a pictograph. Remind students that it is important to match one to one so that the size of objects doesn't affect the rows/columns, therefore making it hard to read the graph. (If desired, tape a grid to the floor so that only one object can fit in each square of the graph.)

5. Ask students to tell which object they found the most of. Model how to look at the graph and find the tallest or longest line of objects. Ask students to tell which has more, the ___ or the ___. Model how to compare two categories of objects. Repeat with similar questions about the pictograph.

Caution: Before beginning any nature activity, ask families' permission and inquire about students' plant and animal allergies. Remind students not to touch plants or animals during the activity.

 Math Talk

Which objects did you collect the most of?
Which objects did you find the same amounts of?
How many more of these did you find than those?

 Journal Prompt

Draw a picture graph for your group's nature collection.

Materials

linking cubes
pattern blocks
graph paper (large squares)
counters (5 colors)
crayons or colored pencils

 Workstations

Activity sheets (pages 137–139)
Grab and Graph (page 140)
Button Sort (page 134)

 Guided Math

⬤ Remediation: Linking Cubes Graph

1. Give each student a set of linking cubes (2 yellow, 5 blue, and 8 red).
2. Have students sort their cubes by color and link them together. When placed on the table side by side, the linking cubes should resemble a bar graph. Do this step with your own set of linking cubes as well.
3. Ask questions based on students' linking cube graphs. Ask, for example, "What color are most of the cubes? How many blue cubes do you have?"
4. Show students how to arrange the linked cubes to compare the heights of the "bars" and to easily compare and answer questions about the number of each color.

▢ On Level: Making Bar Graphs

1. Choose 20 pattern blocks of four different shapes and place them in the center of the group.
2. Have students work together to sort the blocks by shape and arrange them in columns, similar to a pictograph. Show students how three larger shapes (such as hexagons) may make a taller column than five smaller shapes (such as triangles). Ask, "Do the heights of the shape columns relate to the number of shapes? How could we arrange them so they would relate?"
3. Give each student a sheet of graph paper to create a bar graph to reflect the results of the block sort. Show students how to label and align their graphs.
4. Ask questions based on the graphs such as, "What shape has the least number of blocks? Which two shapes have the same number of blocks? How can you tell?"

▲ Enrichment: Tally and Graph

1. Give each student 30 counters in five different colors, a sheet of graph paper, and crayons or colored pencils.
2. Help students make tally charts with the five colors. Then, have students sort their counters by color, making tally marks beside the colors as they count and sort the counters.
3. Show students how to create graphs with labels for each color along the bottoms and numbers along the left sides.
4. Have students transfer the information from their tally charts onto their bar graphs.
5. Ask questions based on the graphs. Ask, for example, "What color on your graph has the most counters?" Have students write their own questions and compare their graphs.

 Assess and Extend

Display a simple graph. Ask students, "If you add one more category to this graph, how many items would you have to have for that category to have the most? The least?"

Graphing Data

Use linking cubes to make the graph shown. Line up the cubes with the picture.

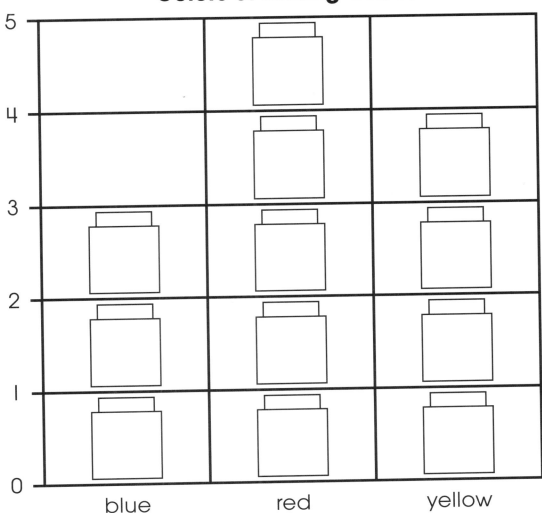

Colors of Linking Cubes

Color the columns of cubes to match the linking cubes.

How many cubes are in each column?

blue _____   red _____   yellow _____

Which color of cubes are there the most of? _____

Which color of cubes are there the least of? _____

Graphing Data ☐ Making Bar Graphs

Use the graph to answer the questions.

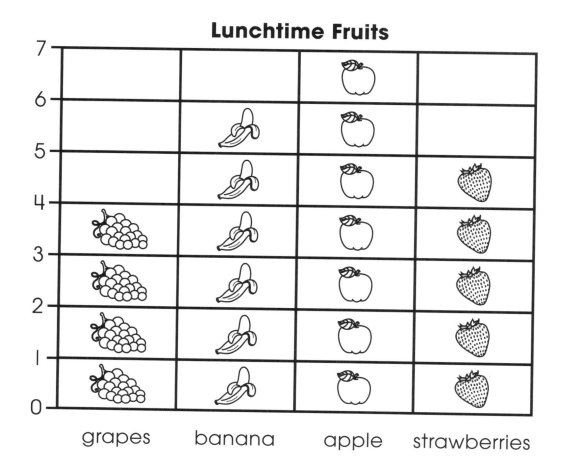

Lunchtime Fruits

How many people had a with lunch? _____

How many people had with lunch? _____

Which fruit did the most people eat? _____

Which fruit did the fewest people eat? _____

How many more people ate a than  ? _____

Graphing Data   ▲ Tally and Graph

Count the shape stickers. Use the tally chart to keep track of the totals. Use the tally chart to help you color the bar graph.

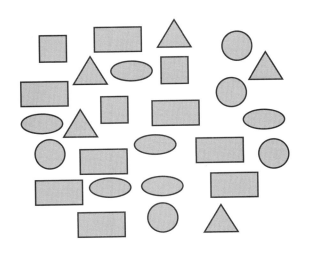

Sticker Shapes

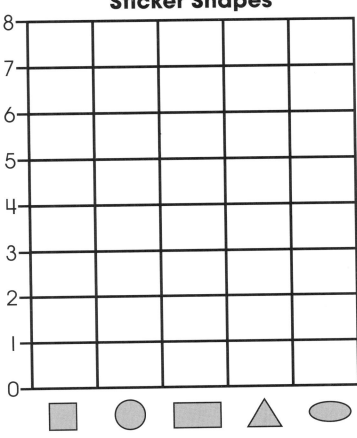

Tally Chart

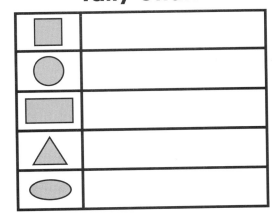

Use the bar graph to answer the questions.

Which 2 shapes have the same number of stickers? _____

Which shape has the most stickers? _____

Which shape has the least stickers? _____

How many more rectangle stickers are there than circle stickers? _____

Grab and Graph

Materials: container of linking cubes

Directions: Take a handful of cubes. Sort the cubes. Count the cubes. Place the cubes on the graph in the correct columns. Read each card aloud. Fill in the blanks with your information.

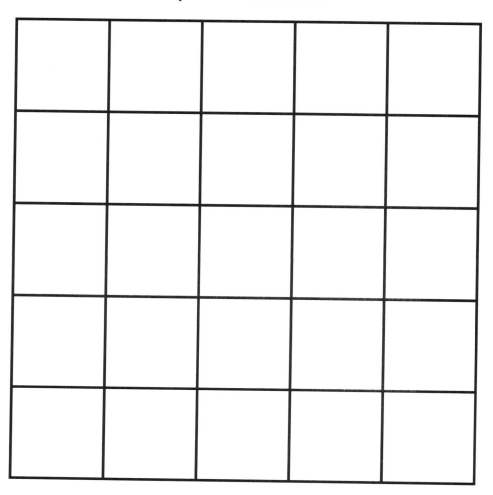

How many red cubes are there?	Are there more red or blue cubes?	Which color has the most?
How many yellow cubes are there?	Are there less yellow or green cubes?	Which color has the least?

To prep: Cut apart the prompt cards. Place the graph and prompt cards in a center with the materials and directions.

Calendar Concepts

Essential Question

How are days of the week and dates shown on a calendar?

Warm-Up/Review

Ask students to raise their hands if they know when a certain holiday is, when their birthdays are, what days they have practice, etc. Tell students that we use a calendar to keep track of special days and to know when important dates are.

Mini-Lesson

Materials: classroom calendar or other large calendar to display, copies of the current month's calendar

1. Use the classroom calendar to formally introduce calendar concepts. Begin by telling students that every calendar tells us what month it is. Have the class work together to name the months of the year. Write the months in a single column on the board off to the side.

2. Say, "We can also use the calendar to see what day it is." Have students name the days of the week and write them in a row across the top of the board (as seen on a calendar).

3. Explain that calendars also tell us what the date is. Define *date* as the number of the day. Have students count aloud as you point to each date on the classroom calendar.

4. Discuss how many days are in a week, and how many months are in a year. Model how to identify dates such as next Tuesday, the second Friday of the month, etc.

5. Give each student a copy of the current month's calendar.

6. Model how to find the dates for yesterday, today, and tomorrow. Challenge students to find the date of the first Monday or the last Saturday.

Math Talk

What happens when we get to the end of the row?
What is the next day and date?
How many days are in this month?
How many Fridays are in this month?

Journal Prompt

Write the days of the week for yesterday, today, and tomorrow.

Materials

calendars from the mini-lesson
days of the week cards (several sets)
months of the year cards (several sets)

 Workstations

Activity sheets (pages 143–145)
Make the Month (page 146)

 Guided Math

◯ Remediation: Basic Calendar Concepts

1. Ask students to bring their calendars from the mini-lesson to the math group.
2. Have students find the month on their calendars and then point to the days of the week as you say them together. Repeat the days of the week several times for reinforcement.
3. Next, have students point to each date as you count together. Say, "Find today's date."
4. Talk about the seasons of the year. Ask, "What season is it in July? October? What season is it at the beginning of the year? What season comes after summer?"

▢ On Level: Days of the Week

1. Using their calendars from the mini-lesson, have students share what they know about reading a calendar. Reinforce concepts as needed.
2. Talk about today's day and date. Ask questions such as, "What day will it be tomorrow? What date was it yesterday?"
3. Have students point to the days of the week on their calendars as you say them together.
4. Give each student a set of days of the week cards. Have students shuffle the cards and then put them in order. Repeat as desired. Ask questions to reinforce day order. Ask, for example, "What day comes after Tuesday? What day comes between Thursday and Saturday?"

▲ Enrichment: Sequence of Days and Months

1. Discuss students' calendars. Talk about today's day and date. Ask questions such as, "What day was it on the 15th? How many days in (month) will you go to school? What is tomorrow's date? How many more days are there until Friday?"
2. Give each student a set of days of the week cards and months of the year cards. Instruct students to shuffle the two decks together, mixing the days and the months. Challenge the group to sort and order the cards appropriately.
3. After students have sequenced all of the cards, ask questions to reinforce month order and concepts of time within the year. Ask, "Which month comes before March? What are the summer months? In what months are your birthdays?"

 Assess and Extend

Have students look at this month's calendar. Have them tell you the current day and date. Have them identify the current month.

Calendar Concepts

Use the key to color the calendar.

Key

Today's date = red
All other dates = yellow

Month = blue
Days of the week = green

February

Sunday	Monday	Tuesday	Wednesday	Thursday	Friday	Saturday
		1	2	3	4	5
6	7	8	9	10	11	12
13	14	15	16	17	18	19
20	21	22	23	24	25	26
27	28					

Calendar Concepts

■ Days of the Week

Write the name of the month. Cut out the days of the week. Glue them in order on the calendar. Number the days with the correct dates.

cut ✂

Tuesday
Saturday
Thursday
Monday
Friday
Sunday
Wednesday

Calendar Concepts   ▲ Sequence of Days and Months

1. Number the days of the week from 1 to 7. The first one has been done for you.

_____ Tuesday

_____ Friday

___**1**___ Sunday

_____ Thursday

_____ Monday

_____ Wednesday

_____ Saturday

2. Number the months of the year from 1 to 12. The first one has been done for you.

_____ June

_____ October

_____ March

_____ December

_____ April

___**1**___ January

_____ August

_____ November

_____ July

_____ May

_____ February

_____ September

Answer the questions about the calendar.

April						
Sunday	Monday	Tuesday	Wednesday	Thursday	Friday	Saturday
	1	2	3	4	5	6
7	8	9	10	11	12	13
14	15	16	17	18	19	20
21	22	23	24	25	26	27
28	29	30				

3. What month is it? _____

4. How many days are in this month? _____

5. What day of the week is the 12th? _____

6. If today is the first Tuesday, what day will it be in 4 days?

_____

Make the Month

Directions: Put the puzzle pieces together to make the calendar.

July

Sunday	Monday	Tuesday	Wednesday	Thursday	Friday	Saturday
			1	2	3	4
5	6	7	8	9	10	11
12	13	14	15	16	17	18
19	20	21	22	23	24	25
26	27	28	29	30	31	

To prep: Make several copies on different colors of cardstock and laminate for durability. Cut the calendar along the solid lines to form puzzle pieces. If desired, cut the calendar puzzle in different ways to create several puzzles for varying levels. For example, you may create a puzzle with each row as a different piece, or create a puzzle with more complex shapes.

Relative Positions

 Essential Question

How can words be used to tell where something is?

 Warm-Up/Review

Ask students to sit on the rug. Then, tell them to sit near a friend. Next, tell them to put their hands above their heads. Finally, tell them to put their hands below their chins. Tell students that we use special words to tell position, such as *on, near, above,* and *below.*

 Mini-Lesson

Materials: box, teddy bear, chart paper, counters, index cards

1. Place a box and a teddy bear on the table. Invite two volunteers to stand near the table.

2. Give the two students directions using positional words and phrases such as *on, in, above, below, under, beside, next to, near, far away from, in front of, behind, between,* and *through.* The directions could be for what to do with their bodies (for example, *stand near the table* or *walk through the door*). Or, the directions could be for what to do with the box and the teddy bear (for example, *put a box between you and the teddy bear* or *put the teddy bear in the box*).

3. Create an anchor chart for positional words. Ask students to recall some of the positional words you used during the activity. Write the words on the chart. For example, *on, in, above, below, under, beside, next to, near, far away from, in front of, behind, between,* and *through.*

4. Give each student a counter and an index card. Give students directions for how to move their counters in relation to their cards. Say, for example, "Put the counter under the card. Put the counter next to the card. Put the counters on the card."

 Math Talk

Which words told where the ___ was?
How are the words similar/different?
What is the opposite of this word?
Which word tells where your pencil is?

 Journal Prompt

What are some positional words that have the same meaning? Draw a picture of the bear and box. Write the two positional words that match the picture.

Materials

plastic cups
counting bears
sets of positional word cards
name cards (see below)
dry-erase boards and markers

 Workstations

Activity sheets (pages 149–151)
Where's the Bear? (page 152)

 Guided Math

⬤ Remediation: Using Positional Words

1. Give each student a plastic cup, two counting bears, and a set of positional word cards.
2. Model for students how to move the bear in relation to the cup according to the word on the card. Display a positional word card. Say, "This word says *under*. I will put the bear under the cup." Have students do the same with their bears and cups.
3. Have each student choose a card and read the word. Then, have students move their bears to show the words. Help as needed.
4. Challenge each student to hide her bear in the classroom and use positional words to help another student find it.

▢ On Level: Positional Clues

1. Before the lesson, write each student's name on an index card and hide all of the cards throughout the classroom. Be sure to record specifically where you hid each card.
2. Explain to students that you have hidden cards with student's names somewhere in the classroom. Give students one direction at a time to help them find their cards. Say, for example, "Antonio, your card is under something in the library. Evelyn, your card is next to something blue." Continue until all students find their cards.
3. Pair students and challenge them to hide each other's name cards. Students should use positional words to help their partners find the positions of their names.

△ Enrichment: Following Directions

1. Give each student a dry-erase board and marker. Show students how to draw a 3 x 3 grid on their dry-erase boards. Discuss where left and right are on the boards. Have students mark their boards with an *L* and an *R* as a reference.
2. Tell students a shape, number, or picture you want them to draw. Say a positional word to tell them where to draw the object. Say, for example, "The circle is in the middle. The number 2 is below the circle. The star is next to the circle. The number 1 is to the left of the number 2," and so on.
3. Once all of the spaces are filled, compare the placement of the numbers on students' boards. Ask students to identify the relative position of each shape, number, or picture. Ask, for example, "Where is the number 1?" (next to the number 3)
4. Challenge students to practice giving clues and drawing objects with partners.

 Assess and Extend

Give students a set of clues that lead to the location of a special object (for example, class pet, class snack, etc.). Use sentences that include positional words. Students should follow the clues to locate the object.

Relative Positions Using Positional Words

Use a word from the word bank to complete each sentence.

between	in	in front of	next to	on	under

1.   The teddy bear is _____ the box.

2.   The teddy bear is _____ the box.

3.   The teddy bear is _____

_____ the box.

4.   The teddy bear is _____

_____ _____ the box.

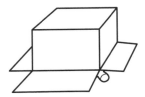

5.   The teddy bear is _____ the box.

6.   The teddy bear is _____ the boxes.

Relative Positions

Read the clues. Color the books to find where the green book is hiding.

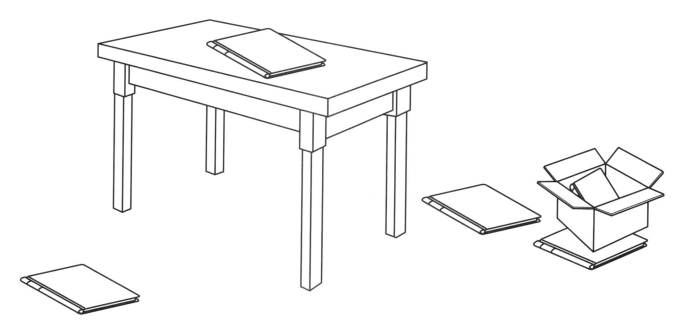

Clues

The red book is on something.
The blue book is next to something.
The brown book is in something.
The orange book is under something.

Color the green book. Describe where it is.

_____

_____

_____

_____

_____

_____

_____

Relative Positions   ▲ Following Directions

Follow the directions to complete the picture.

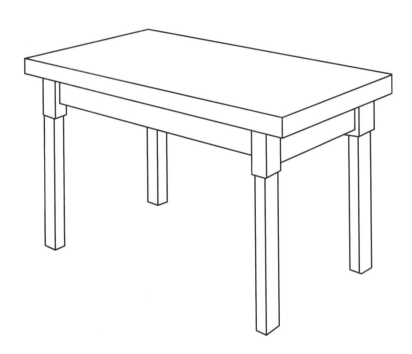

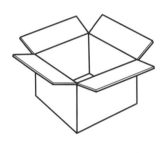

Draw a 🌙 above the box.

Draw a ◯ in the box.

Draw a △ between the table and the box.

Draw a ♡ near the box.

Draw a 🙂 under the table.

Draw a ☐ on the table.

Draw a ☆ to the left of the table.

Is the box to the right or the left of the table? _____

Where's the Bear?

Materials: counting bear, small box

To play: Players take turns. Player 1 takes a position word card and hides the bear. She chooses two more position word cards and lays them out. Player 2 must find the bear and choose the card that describes the position of the bear.

under	on
next to	beside
near	far from
over	beneath
in	in front of
behind	through

The bear is ⬜ the box.

To prep: Copy on card stock and laminate if desired for durability. Cut apart the words and prompt card. Place the cards in a center with the materials and directions.

Shapes

Warm-Up/Review

Place enough pattern blocks or attribute blocks in a bag for each student to have one. Have each student reach into the bag and pull out a block. Have students share what they know about the blocks. Ask, "How can you describe the blocks? How can you tell them apart?"

 Mini-Lesson

Materials: paper shapes (see below), chart paper

1. Before the lesson, place paper circles, triangles, squares, and rectangles of various colors around the classroom. Be sure that the shapes are visible from students' seats.

2. Tell students that shapes are all around them. Point out the shapes that you have hidden around the classroom.

3. Play I Spy by having students look for shapes of specific colors. Begin the game by saying, for example, "I spy a blue circle." Have the student who sees the shape first collect the shape and "spy" the next shape.

4. Once students find all of the shapes, tell students with circles to stand in one corner of the room, students with triangles in another, and so on. Ask each group to share observations about their shapes.

5. Create an anchor chart for students to reference for all of the 2-D shape lessons. Draw each shape and label it. Say, "Some shapes have special names. Look at my chart. This is a circle. It is round. This is a rectangle. It has four straight sides. This is a triangle. It has three sides. This is a square. It has four straight sides that are the same length." Add shapes to the chart as you teach them.

 Math Talk

Can you find something in the classroom that is a circle (square, triangle, etc.)?
How many sides does this shape have?
How many angles does this shape have?
How are these two shapes similar?

 Journal Prompt

Explain how two triangles can look different but still be the same shape.

Materials

shape index cards (see below)
large shape cards (see below)
gallon-sized resealable plastic bags
    with colored hair gel (see below)
pattern blocks

 Workstations

Activity sheets (pages 155–157)
Making Shapes (page 158)

 Guided Math

⬤ Remediation: Matching Shapes

1. Before the lesson, draw on index cards four of each shape: circle, triangle, rectangle, and square. Place the cards facedown on the table.
2. Choose two cards and hold them up. Model how to say each name and say if they match. Be sure to give reasons why the shapes match or do not match.
3. Collect, shuffle, and place the cards facedown on the table in a 4 x 4 array. Have each student take turns flipping over two cards. Have the student say the name of the shapes she is holding while showing them to the group. If the shapes match, she keeps the pair. If the shapes do not match, she flips the cards back over. Make sure that she explains her reasoning. Have students continue to play until they have matched all of the cards.

⬜ On Level: Identifying and Drawing Shapes

1. Before the lesson, draw or print on cardstock an example of each of the following: circle, square, triangle, rectangle, trapezoid, and hexagon.
2. Display the shapes. Review the shapes names learned in the group lesson. Teach the trapezoid and hexagon. Discuss their attributes.
3. Give each student a large shape card and a resealable plastic bag filled with colored hair gel. (Squeeze out all extra air before sealing, and use clear packing tape to reinforce the seal on the plastic bag.) Have students place their bags over the shape cards. Model how to trace the shapes using their fingers. Have students switch shape cards and repeat.
4. Have students share what they notice about the shapes. Prompt by asking about the types of lines (curved or straight) and number of lines and corners used to form each shape.

△ Enrichment: Polygons

1. Place pattern blocks on the table. Introduce the word *polygon* (a shape with many straight sides). Ask, "Are circles polygons? Why or why not?" (No, they don't have straight sides.) Together, identify the names of the various polygons. Teach the names of those shapes the students may not know, such as rhombuses, trapezoids, parallelograms, and hexagons.
2. Have students trace and label each block on their papers.
3. Have students use pattern blocks to find multiple ways to create a triangle, a square, a rectangle, and other polygons. Have students record their discoveries by tracing the shapes on their papers.

 Assess and Extend

Have each student make a small and a large triangle with pattern blocks. Then, have students try to make congruent shapes with different blocks.

Shapes   ● Matching Shapes

Use the key to color the matching shapes.

Key

triangle = yellow   circle = blue
square = red   rectangle = green

Shapes

Trace each shape. Draw each shape.

circle	rectangle
triangle	square
trapezoid	hexagon

Shapes   Polygons

1. Draw a line from each shape to the correct shape word.

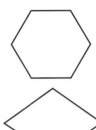   trapezoid

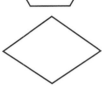   hexagon

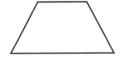   parallelogram

   rhombus

2. Use pattern blocks to cover the hexagons. Trace and color the shapes to show what blocks you used.

I block	2 matching blocks	3 matching blocks
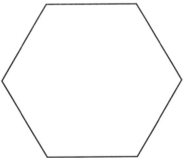	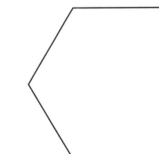	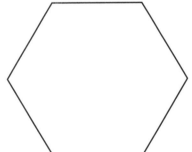

3 different blocks	6 matching blocks	Can you find another way?
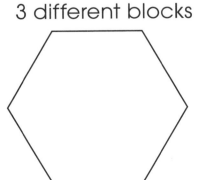	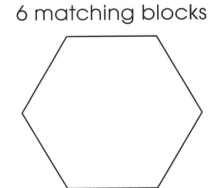	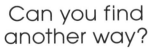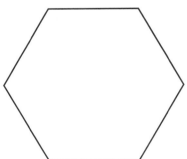

Making Shapes

Materials: wax-coated string, trays

Directions: Choose a card. Use string to make the shape.

Make a △.	Make a triangle.
Make a ◯.	Make a square.
Make a □.	Make a rectangle.
Make a ▭.	Make a trapezoid.
Make a hexagon.	Make a rhombus.
Make a 3-sided shape. Can you make it in a different way?	Make a 5-sided shape. Can you make it in a different way?
Make a 4-sided shape. Can you make it in a different way?	Make a 6-sided shape. Can you make it in a different way?

To prep: Copy on card stock and laminate if desired for durability. Cut apart the cards. Place them in a center with the materials and directions. To differentiate, choose different cards for each leveled group.

Solid Shapes

 Warm-Up/Review

Create a graphic organizer on the board with the word *shapes* in the middle. Ask students to tell you everything they know about shapes. List their responses on the board and discuss their ideas.

 Mini-Lesson

Materials: real-world 3-D objects (for example, die, ball, traffic cone, and can), chart paper

1. Tell students that three-dimensional, or solid shapes, are all around them. Hold up a die. Say, "This die is a cube." Hold up a can. Ask students to share if they know what shape it is. Continue with a ball and a traffic cone. Discuss how 2-D and 3-D shapes are different.

2. Create a chart for students to reference for all of the 3-D shape lessons. Draw the shape and label it. Say, "Some shapes have special names. Look at the chart. This is a sphere. It is round. This is a cube. It has six flat, square faces. This is a cylinder. It is round and has two flat faces that are circles. This is a cone. It has one flat face that is a circle." Add shapes to the chart as you teach them.

3. Play I Spy by having students look for solid shapes around the classroom. Begin the game by saying, for example, "I spy a blue sphere." Have the student who spies the shape first give the next clue.

4. Have students share observations about the shapes that they spied.

 Math Talk

Can you find something in the classroom that is a sphere (cube, cone, etc.)? How many faces does this shape have? How are these two shapes similar?

 Journal Prompt

Find two examples of solid shapes in the classroom. Give reasons why the objects are both that shape.

Materials

shape cards (see below)
real-world three-dimensional object
    cards (see below)
three-dimensional shape blocks

 Workstations

Activity sheets (pages 161–163)
Spin and Color (page 164)

 Guided Math

⃝ **Remediation: Matching Solid Shapes**

1. Before the lesson, draw on index cards four of each shape: sphere, cube, cone, and cylinder. Place them facedown on the table.
2. Choose two cards and hold them up. Model how to say each name and say if they match. Be sure to give reasons why the shapes match or do not match.
3. Collect, shuffle, and place the cards facedown on the table in a 4 x 4 array. Have each student take turns flipping over two cards. Have each student say the name of the shapes that she is holding while showing them to the group. If the shapes match, he keeps the pair. If the shapes do not match, he flips the cards back over. Students should be able to justify their reasonings. Students should continue to play until they have matched all of the cards.

▢ **On Level: Identifying Solid Shapes**

1. Before the lesson, draw on index cards four of each shape: sphere, cube, cone, and cylinder and two of each real-world examples of these shapes. Place them facedown on the table.
2. Choose two cards and hold them up. Model how to say each name and say if they match. Be sure to give reasons why the shapes match or do not match.
3. Collect, shuffle, and place the cards facedown on the table in a 4 x 6 array. Have each student take turns flipping over two cards. If the cards show the same shape (solid shape and/or real-world shape), she keeps the pair. If the shapes are not the same, she flips the cards back over. Students should be able to justify their reasonings. Students should continue to play until they have matched all of the cards.

△ **Enrichment: Attributes of Solid Shapes**

1. Place on the table one of each of the following blocks: sphere, cube, cone, and cylinder. Review with students the shape names learned in the group lesson. Discuss their attributes and review the terms *face, edge,* and *vertex (vertices)*.
2. Give each student a sheet of paper and a pencil. Model how to trace one of the block's faces.
3. Have each student choose one block and trace the faces of the solid on his paper. (Remove spheres for this part of the lesson.) Have students hold up their papers and describe what they notice about their shapes.

 Assess and Extend

Have each student draw a picture of objects in the classroom that are solid shapes. Students should label their pictures with the correct shape names.

Solid Shapes

⬤ Matching Solid Shapes

Cut out the shapes. Glue them next to the shapes that match. Write one thing you know about each shape.

1.  _____

_____

2. 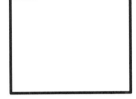 _____

_____

3.  _____

_____

4.  _____

_____

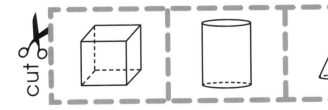

cut

Solid Shapes   Identifying Solid Shapes

Solid figures are three-dimensional figures.

 cube   sphere   cone   pyramid   cylinder

Name the solid figure that each object looks like.

1.

_____

2.

_____

3.

_____

4.

_____

5.

_____

6.

_____

7.

_____

8.

_____

9.

_____

Solid Shapes   ▲ Attributes of Solid Shapes

Draw the flat faces of each shape.

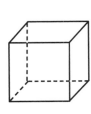   

   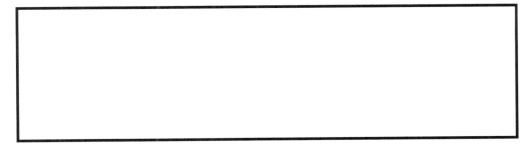

Write a sentence that tells how a cone and a cylinder
are alike.

_____

_____

_____

_____

Spin and Color

Materials: sharpened pencil, paper clip, two colors of crayons

To play: Each player chooses a color of crayon. Players take turns. Use the pencil and paper clip to spin the spinner. Color a matching shape or object on the game board. If no shapes are left, you lose a turn. The player who has the most shapes colored wins.

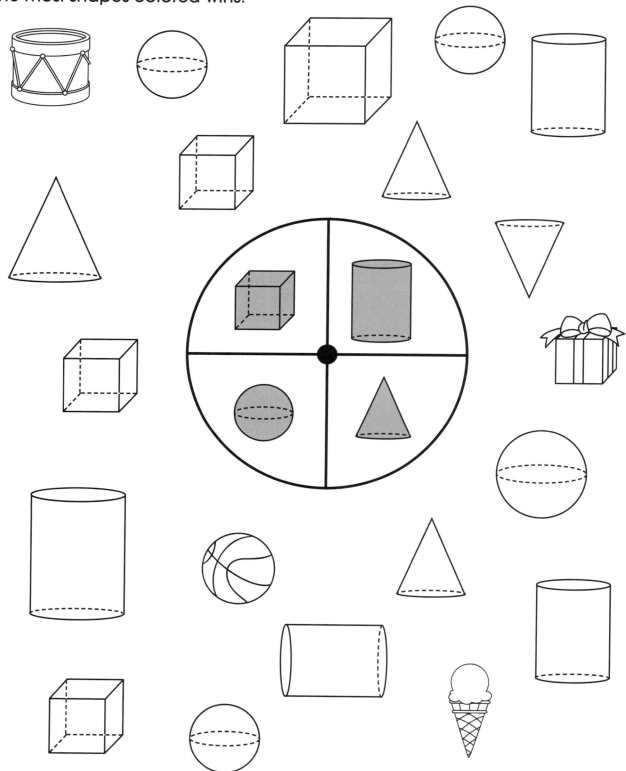

Flat vs. Solid Shapes

 ## Essential Question

How are flat and solid shapes different?

Warm-Up/Review

Show students a game board. Remind students that flat shapes all lay in the same plane like a space on a game board. Hold up the game board at eye level so that students can see that it is flat and that no spaces can be seen. Solid shapes have dimension like a playing piece on a game board. Place a game piece on the board and hold it at eye level. Students should be able to see the game piece standing upright on the board.

 ## Mini-Lesson

Materials: flat and solid shape blocks, bag

1. Before the lesson, put the flat and solid shape blocks in a bag.

2. Have a few students reach into the bag and try to pull out either a "flat" shape or a "solid" shape. Ask students to share how they know that they are choosing the right kind of shape. (For example, flat blocks lay on the floor and solid shapes stand upright on the floor.)

3. Give each student a flat and a solid shape block. Have students feel the shapes in their hands and explore how the two shapes are different. Have students share what they notice that is similar and different about the shapes.

 ## Math Talk

Can you find a shape that is similar to the face of this solid shape?
Which shapes can you stack?
Which shapes can you roll?

 ## Journal Prompt

Explain how a cube and a square are the same and different.

Materials

paper
flat and solid shape blocks
laminated sorting mats (see below)
flat and solid shape picture cards
paper squares (such as origami paper)
tape

 Workstations

Activity sheets (pages 167–169)
Sorting Shapes (page 170)
Spin and Color (page 164)
Making Shapes (page 158)

 Guided Math

⚪ **Remediation: Flat or Solid?**

1. Give each student a sheet of paper. Have students lay the paper on the table. Have students look at the table at eye level. Tell them that the paper is flat. Ask them to identify which shape it is. (rectangle)

2. Have students take the paper and crumple it into a ball. Have them lay the paper on the table. Ask, "What do you notice about the paper now? Does it lay flat?" Have students look at the table at eye level and see that the paper now comes off the table and has height. Tell students that the balled up paper is like a sphere. It has dimension, or takes up space above the table, not only on the table.

3. Give students flat and solid shape blocks to explore. Have students look at the shapes from eye level and discuss which shapes have dimension.

🔲 **On Level: Sorting Shapes**

1. Give each student a set of flat and solid shape blocks and a sorting mat. Have students sort the blocks on the mats. Ask students to give reasons for their sorting.

2. Have students remove the blocks and give each student flat and solid shape picture cards. Have students sort the pictures by flat or solid shape. Tell students that although the pictures are flat, some of the objects show dimension.

3. Challenge students to find objects in the classroom that are flat or solid and sort them on the mats.

🔺 **Enrichment: Flat Shapes on Solid Shapes**

1. Give each student a solid shape block (including prisms and pyramids). Have each student trace the faces of the solid shape.

2. Tell students that some solid shapes have flat shapes on their faces. Ask students to name the flat shapes made by tracing the sides.

3. Give each student six equal-sized paper squares, tape, and a solid shape block cube. Challenge students to tape the squares together to create cubes. Help as needed.

 Assess and Extend

Have students find one solid and one flat object in the classroom. Have students tell one thing that is the same and one thing that is different about the shapes.

Flat vs. Solid Shapes ● Flat or Solid?

Color the flat shapes red. Color the solid shapes blue.

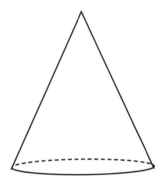

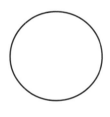
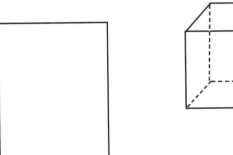
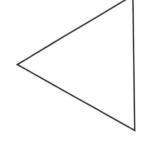

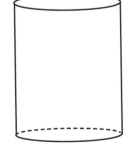
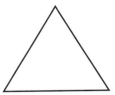

Flat vs. Solid Shapes Sorting Shapes

Cut out the shapes. Glue each shape under the correct heading.

Flat Shapes	**Solid Shapes**

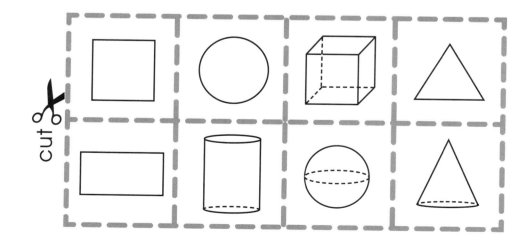

cut

Date _____

Draw a line to match each solid shape to the flat shape(s) of its faces. Some shapes will have more than one face shape.

1.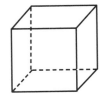

2.

3.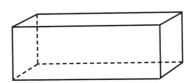

4.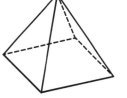

5.

6.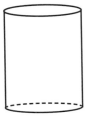

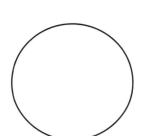

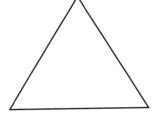

Sorting Shapes

Materials: picture cards, sorting mat

Directions: Lay out the picture cards. Sort them on the mat.

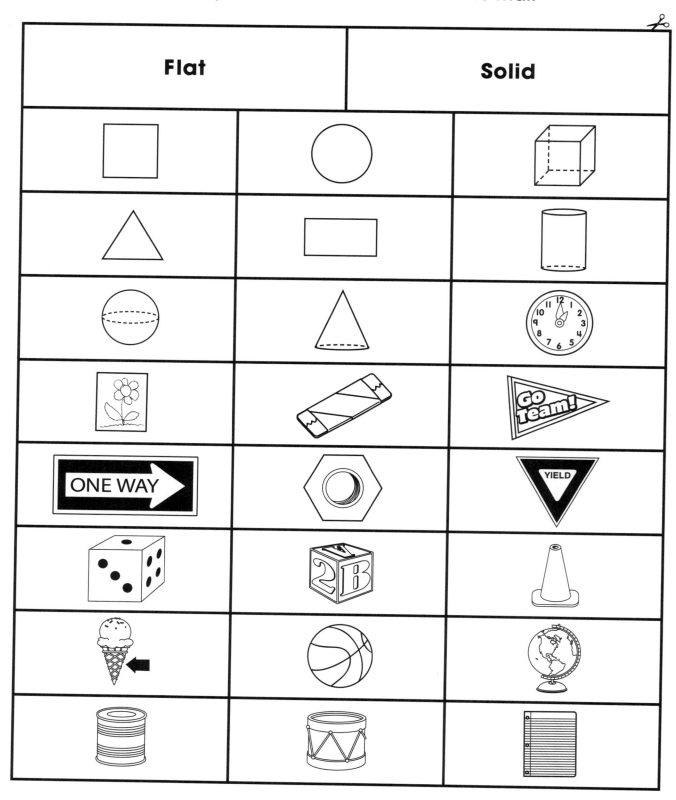

To prep: Copy on card stock for durability. Glue each header to each side of an open file folder to create the sorting mat. Cut apart the cards. Place the game in a center with the sorting mat and directions.

Shape Attributes

Essential Question

How are two-dimensional and three-dimensional shapes alike and different?

Warm-Up/Review

Hold up a sheet of paper and a cereal box. Have students tell what they notice about each one. Point out the rectangular faces of the cereal box. Tell students that they will learn the words to describe the parts of each shape.

Mini-Lesson

Materials: chart paper, colored markers

1. Before the lesson, draw a large square and a large cube on chart paper. Display the chart.
2. Have students identify the square. Write the shape name under the square.
3. Have students come to the chart and use a colored marker to trace each side of the square. Label one *side*. Have students come to the chart and use a different color to circle the angles, or where two sides meet. Label one *angle*.
4. Next, have students identify the cube. Write the shape name under the cube.
5. Have students come to the chart and use a colored marker to trace each edge of the cube. Label one *edge*. Have students come to the chart and use a different color to circle the vertices, or where three edges meet. Label one *vertex*. Have one student come to the chart and use a third color to shade in one face. Label one *face*.
6. Have students count the attributes of each shape and list the numbers below each label.

Math Talk

How are a side and an edge alike? Different?

How are an angle and a vertex alike? Different?

How many sides and angles are on this shape?

How many edges, vertices, and faces are on this shape?

Journal Prompt

Explain how a side and an edge are the same and different.

Materials

attribute blocks
crayons
solid shape blocks
printed copies of solid shapes
shape name cards
dry-erase boards and markers

 Workstations

Activity sheets (pages 173–175)
Sort It Out! (page 176)
Sorting Shapes (page 170)
Spin and Color (page 164)
Making Shapes (page 158)

 Guided Math

⭕ **Remediation: Attributes of Flat Shapes**

1. Give each student one of each attribute block and crayons.
2. Have students trace the blocks onto sheets of paper. Have them use different colors of crayons to trace each side of the shape. For example, students would use three colors to trace the sides of the triangle. Have students label one *side*.
3. Have students use black crayons to circle all of the shapes' angles. Have students label one *angle*.
4. Challenge students to point out which shapes have the least and most sides and angles.

🟦 **On Level: Attributes of Solid Shapes**

1. Give each student a cube. Model for students how to draw the shape.
2. Have students draw the cube on a sheet of paper. Have them use a different color crayon to trace each edge. Have students shade in one face. Have students label one *edge* and one *face*. Have students use a black crayon to circle all of the vertices on the shapes. Have students label one *vertex*.
3. Challenge students to point out what they notice about the number of faces, edges, and vertices on a cube.
4. Repeat with printed copies of other solid shapes. Emphasize that curved surfaces and edges are not true faces or edges. They must be flat and straight to be a face or an edge. So, a cone only has one face and no edges. A cylinder has two faces and no edges. A sphere has no faces or edges.

🔺 **Enrichment: Identifying Shape Attributes**

1. Place several flat and solid shape blocks on the table. Have students use the shape name cards to identify the shapes.
2. Tell students that you are going to read some clues about a shape. Say, "This shape has four equal-length sides." Students should write *square* on their dry-erase boards. Students should hold up their boards for you to check for understanding.
3. Repeat with other shapes, giving clues about the number of sides, edges, faces, angles, and vertices.

 Assess and Extend

Have students find two pictures in catalogs or magazines that show related flat and solid shapes such as a circle and a cone. Have students explain how the two shapes are related. (For example, *The cone has a circular face.*)

172 © Carson-Dellosa • CD-104952

Shape Attributes ● Attributes of Flat Shapes

Complete the chart.

Shape	Sides	Angles
▢	_____	_____
△	_____	_____
▭	_____	_____
(trapezoid)	_____	_____
(parallelogram)	_____	_____
(hexagon)	_____	_____

Shape Attributes   ☐ Attributes of Solid Shapes

Complete the chart.

Shape	Faces	Edges	Vertices
☐ (cube)	_____	_____	_____
(cylinder)	_____	_____	_____
(cone)	_____	_____	_____
(sphere)	_____	_____	_____
(rectangular prism)	_____	_____	_____
(triangular prism)	_____	_____	_____
(pyramid)	_____	_____	_____

Shape Attributes   ▲ Identifying Shape Attributes

Circle the shape that matches each clue.

1. I have 3 angles and 3 sides.

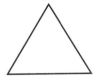   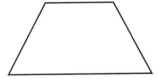

2. I have 6 faces.

3. I have 4 angles.

4. I have 1 flat face.

5. I have 4 angles and 4 equal-length sides.

Sort It Out!

Materials: sorting mat, cards, shape blocks
Directions: Choose a sorting mat. Sort the blocks under the correct heading on the mat.

Roll	Stack

2-D (Flat)	3-D (Solid)

4 Corners	4 or More Corners

3 Sides	4 or More Sides

4 or Less Faces	5 or More Faces

To prep: Copy on cardstock for durability. Glue each pair of headers to each side of an open file folder to create five sorting mats. Place the mats in a center with the materials and directions.

Composing Shapes

Essential Question

What are some ways to compose shapes?

Warm-Up/Review

Have students see if they can use their bodies to make shapes. Lead students through exercises that stretch their bodies to make shapes. Pair students to make larger shapes.

Mini-Lesson

Materials: sheets of square paper (such as origami paper)

1. Give each student three sheets of square paper.

2. Have each student hold up one sheet of paper and tell what shape it is (square). Tell students that they are going to make other shapes from this square. Have students fold one sheet of paper in half horizontally. Have them open their papers and see that two small rectangles make the square.

3. Have each student take a second sheet of paper and fold it in half twice. Have students open the paper and see that four small squares make the larger square.

4. Have each student take the third sheet of paper and fold it in half on the diagonal. Have students open the paper and see that two triangles make the larger square.

5. Challenge each student to fold one sheet of paper again and see what other shapes compose the larger square. Allow students to share their observations.

Math Talk

If we fold this shape, what smaller shapes make the larger shape?

What shapes could this shape be made from?

What do you predict will happen if I fold the paper like this?

Journal Prompt

Draw a square. Explain how both triangles and rectangles can be put together to make squares.

Materials

pattern blocks (remove squares and tan, skinny rhombuses)

 Workstations

Activity sheets (pages 179–181)
Hex-a-Go! (page 182)

 Guided Math

⭕ **Remediation: Composing Shapes from Triangles**
1. Place a set of pattern blocks on the table. Tell students that they are going to find ways to use triangles to make the larger blocks.
2. Give students time to explore using the blocks. Then, have each student place a rhombus (parallelogram), a trapezoid, and a hexagon on the table. Have students cover the blocks with triangles.
3. Ask students to share how many blocks they used to cover each shape.

🟦 **On Level: Composing Hexagons**
1. Place a set of pattern blocks on the table and ask students to take one hexagon block each. Tell students that they are going to find the ways to compose a hexagon from smaller blocks.
2. Give students time to explore using the blocks. Then, have each student try to use just one type of block to cover the hexagon.
3. Challenge students to try to use two different types of blocks to cover the hexagon.

🔺 **Enrichment: Composing Larger Shapes**
1. Place a set of pattern blocks on the table. Tell students that they are going to find ways to compose larger shapes from smaller shapes.
2. Have each student use four shapes to compose a larger shape. Have students share what they were able to make. Ask, "How many sides and angles does the new shape have?"
3. Challenge students to find two ways to compose the same shape.

 Assess and Extend

Ask students, "What is the least amount of blocks needed to make a large triangle?"

Composing Shapes ● Composing Shapes from Triangles

Follow the directions.

1. Make and draw a shape using 2 △s.	**2.** Make and draw a shape using 3 △s.
3. Make and draw a shape using 6 △s.	**4.** Write a number. Make and draw a shape using that number of △s. _____

Composing Shapes   ■ Composing Hexagons

Circle the group of shapes that make each hexagon. Draw the shapes inside the hexagon.

1.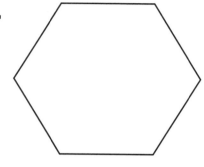

  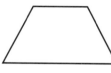

 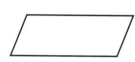 

2.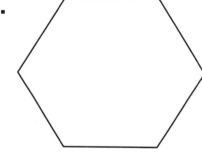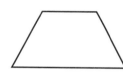

 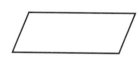

3.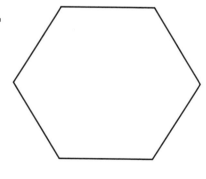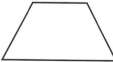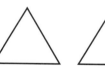

 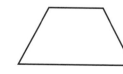

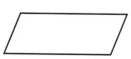

Composing Shapes

Fill in each parallelogram a different way. Trace the blocks you use inside the larger shape.

Hex-a-Go!

Materials: sharpened pencil, paper clip, pattern blocks

To play: Players take turns. Use the sharpened pencil and paper clip to spin the spinner. Take that block. Put it on the first hexagon. Add the shapes you spin to your hexagons until they are full. The first player to fill all of her hexagons wins.

Start

Finish

To prep: Copy on card stock and laminate if desired for durability. Place the game board in a center with the materials and directions.

Color it.

Number of the Day

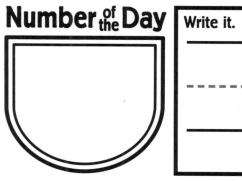

Write it.

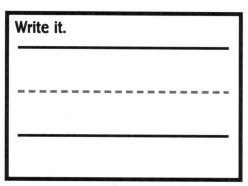

Tally it.

Show it on the ten frames.

Draw it.

If there are more than 10, circle 10.

_____ ten _____ ones

Make a number bond.

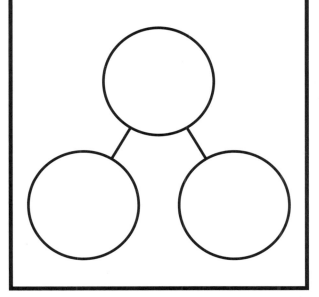

Count on.

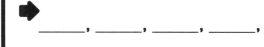 _____, _____, _____, _____, _____

Count back.

_____, _____, _____, _____, _____

Materials: 2 dice, 10 counters (in two colors) per player

To play: Players take turns. Roll the dice and _____ .
Cover the answer. You can "bump" the other player off of a space if there is only one counter on it. Once you place two counters on a space, it is yours and cannot be bumped. The player to use all of his or her counters first wins.

BUMP!

- ✂

To prep: Complete the title with the skill. Fill in the spaces with possible answers. Complete the directions with instructions related to the skill that describe how students use the numbers they roll. For example, *multiply the numbers* or *add, then cover the number that is two less*. Cut these directions off before copying. If desired, copy on cardstock and laminate for durability. Place it in a station with the related materials.

_____ Four-in-a-Row

Materials: _____ dice, two different colors of counters

To play: Players take turns. _____
_____. Place your counter on
the answer. If a counter is already on a space, you may not place a counter on the same
space. The first player with four counters in a row wins.

○ ○ ○ ○ ○ ○

○ ○ ○ ○ ○ ○

○ ○ ○ ○ ○ ○

○ ○ ○ ○ ○ ○

○ ○ ○ ○ ○ ○

○ ○ ○ ○ ○ ○

- ✂

To prep: Fill in the circles with numbers. Place the numbers in random order and repeat numbers throughout. Fill in the number of dice needed in the Materials section. Complete the directions with instructions specific to the skill. For example, _roll two dice and add the numbers,_ or _roll three dice, place the numbers in any order to create a three-digit number, and round it to the nearest ten._ Cut off these directions before copying. If desired, copy it on cardstock and laminate for durability. Place it in a station with the related materials.

Path Game

Materials: 1 die, 1 marker or game piece for each player

To play: Players take turns. Roll the die. Move forward that many spaces. Solve the problem or follow the instructions on the space. If using cards, draw a card and solve the problem. If you answer correctly, stay on the space. If you answer incorrectly, return to your previous space. The first player to reach the Finish space wins.

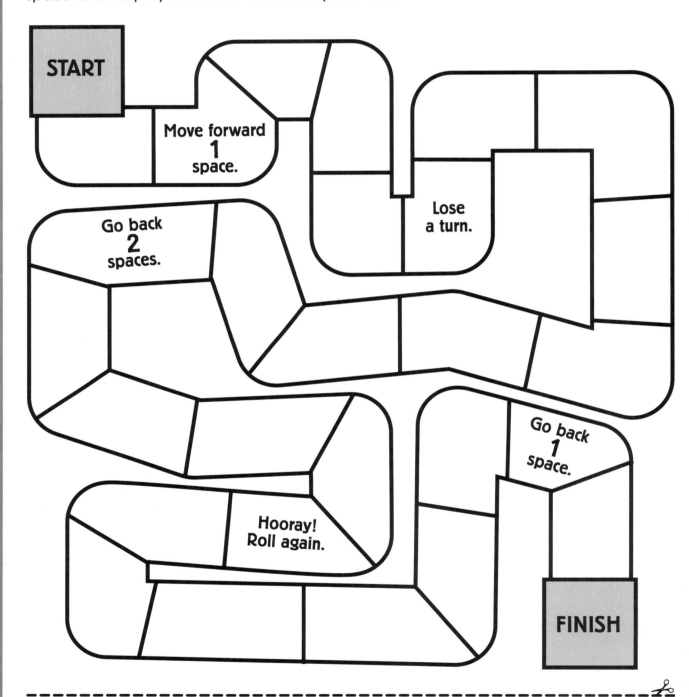

START

Move forward
1
space.

Go back
2
spaces.

Lose
a turn.

Go back
1
space.

Hooray!
Roll again.

FINISH

To prep: Fill in the title with a fun or skill-based name. If using cards, add them to the materials list and create cards with problems or prompts on cardstock or index cards. If not using cards, write problems directly on the blank spaces. Cut off these directions before copying. If desired, copy them on cardstock and laminate for durability. Place them in a station with the related materials.

_____ Roll and Solve

Materials: I die

To play: Roll the die. Find the matching column and solve the bottom problem. Continue rolling and solving the next problem in each column until one column is complete. Color the winning animal. Continue to see which animals win second and third place.

To prep: Complete the title with the skill. Fill in the spaces below each animal with different problems. Cut off these directions before copying. If desired, copy them on cardstock and laminate for durability. Place them in a station with the related materials.

_____ Flip!

To play: Shuffle the cards. Place them all facedown. Players take turns. The first player flips over one card and _____ _____. If the player answers correctly, he may keep the card. If not, return the card facedown to the pile. Once all of the cards have been flipped, the player with the most cards wins.

To prep: Complete the title with the skill. Fill in the cards with numbers or other prompts, such as geometric figures, angles, or shapes. Complete the directions by telling how students should answer or solve the prompts on the cards. For example, *tell what type of angle is shown,* or *tell how many to add to make 10.* Copy the cards on cardstock for durability and laminate if desired. Place them in a center with the directions. You may include a spatula and paper plates with the activity for students to use when "flipping" the cards and maintaining their "keep" piles.

_____ Shut the Box

Materials: _____ dice, _____ counters per person

To play: Cover all of the spaces on your board with markers. Players take turns. Roll the dice. _____

If it has already been uncovered, mark one of your strikes. After one player has gotten three strikes, the player who has removed the most counters wins. Or, the first player to remove all of the counters without getting three strikes wins.

Player 1

Strike ① ② ③

Strike ① ② ③

Player 2

✂ -

To prep: Complete the title with the skill. Fill in the spaces on each section with the possible answers. Both sections should have the same numbers. You do not have to fill in all of the spaces. Complete the materials section with the number of dice and counters needed. Complete the directions with instructions related to the skill that describe how students use the numbers they roll. For example, _double the number, then uncover the answer,_ or _add, then uncover the sum._ Cut off these directions before copying. If desired, copy them on cardstock and laminate for durability. Place them in a station with the related materials.

Answer Key

Page 17
1. 1; 2. 3; 3. 5; 4. 2; 5. 5; 6. 4

Page 18
1. 8; 2. 7; 3. 9; 4. 6; 5. 4

Page 19
Numbers should appear in order from 1 to 20.

Page 23
1. 30; 2. 50; 3. 20; 4. 10; 5. 40

Page 24
1. 50; 2. 30; 3. 40; 4. 80; 5. 60

Page 25
1. Students should color 1–10 yellow. 2. Students should color 10, 20, 30, 40, 50, 60, 70, 80, 90, and 100 red. 3. Students should color 5, 10, 15, 20, 25, 30, 35, 40, 45, 50, 55, 60, 65, 70, 75, 80, 85, 90, 95, and 100 blue. Answers will vary.

Page 29
Answers will vary.

Page 30
Answers will vary.

Page 31
1. 3, 16, 13, 7; 2. 11, 5, 19, 8; 3. 7, 1, 13, 16

Page 35
Check students' work.

Page 36
1. 1; 2. 3; 3. 4; 4. 6; 5. 7; 6. 9

Page 37
Check students' work.

Page 41
Check students' work. 1. 3; 2. 5; 3. 2; 4. 7; 5. 4

Page 42
Check students' work.

Page 43
Check students' work.

Page 44
A. 6; B. 4; C. 9; D. 12; E. 15; F. 17

Page 47
1. Check students' work.
2. 2, 4, 3

Page 48
1. Check students' work.
2. 10, 7, 5, 8; Check students' work.

Page 49
1. Check students' work.
2. 15, 17

Page 53
1. 4 cats; 2. 8 balloons; 3. 7 balls; 4. 5 dogs; 5. 6 flowers

Page 54
1. 4 yellow, 6 red; 2. 8 blue, 9 red; 3. 10 red, 6 yellow; 4. 7 red, 6 blue; 5. 6 red, 4 blue

Page 55
Check students' work.

Page 59
From top to bottom, left to right: 4; 3; 5; 4; 5; 2; 5; 4; 5; 3; 4; 4

Page 60
From top to bottom, left to right: 6; 7; 8; 9; 6; 2; 8; 7; 6; 7; 8; 9

Page 61
1. <, <, >; 2. <, >, <; 3. <, <, >; 4. >. <, <; 5. >, >, <

Page 65
1. 3, 2; 2. 1, 4; 3. 4, 1; 4. 2, 3

Page 66
Answers will vary.

Page 67
1. 3 + 3 = 6; 2. 6 + 2 = 8; 3. 4 + 5 = 9; 4. 7 + 3 = 10; 5. Answers will vary.

Page 71
1. 3; 2. 3; 3. 3; 4. 2; 5. 2

Page 72
1. 3; 2. 3; 3. 3; 4. 1; 5. 6; 6. 6

Page 73
1. 5 – 2 = 3; 2. 8 – 3 = 5; 3. 4 – 2 = 2; 4. 9 – 4 = 5; 5. 7 – 3 = 4; 6. 5 – 1 = 4

Page 77
1. 7; 2. 6; 3. 5; 4. 7

Page 78
Check students' work. 1. 6; 2. 7; 3. 5; 4. 4

Page 79
1. 5 + 1 = 6; 2. 3 + 4 = 7; 3. 4 + 4 = 8; 4. 2 + 6 = 8; 5. 7 + 2 = 9; 6. 6 + 3 = 9

Answer Key

Page 80
A. 8 apples; B. 6 balloons;
C. 6 trucks; D. 10 bracelets;
E. 9 windows; F. 10 seashells;
G. 9 pets; H. 8 books

Page 83
1. 3; 2. 6; 3. 2; 4. 6

Page 84
Check students' work. 1. 4; 2. 1;
3. 7; 4. 3

Page 85
1. 6 – 1 = 5; 2. 8 – 4 = 4;
3. 4 – 1 = 3; 4. 7 – 6 = 1;
5. 9 – 7 = 2; 6. 5 – 1 = 4

Page 86
A. 2 pies; B. 4 pens; C. 6 ice
cubes; D. 3 baseballs;
E. 3 bracelets; F. 6 seashells;
G. 3 bones; H. 3 beads

Page 89
1. Check students' work.
2. 3, 4, 2

Page 90
1. Answers will vary. Check
students' work. 2. 6, 7, 5

Page 91
Answers will vary.

Page 95
Check students' work. 1. 7; 2. 5;
3. 1; 4. 4; 5. 8; 6. 3; 7. 6; 8. 0;
9. 9; 10. 2

Page 96
Check students' work. 1. 6; 2. 3;
3. 8; 4. 10; 5. 5; 6. 1

Page 97
Answers will vary.

Page 101
1. AB; 2. ABB; 3. AAB; 4. ABC;
Answers will vary.

Page 102
1. triangle, square;
2. triangle, circle, square;
3. square, circle, circle;
4. circle, circle, triangle;
5. square, circle, square;
6. triangle, square, square

Page 103
Check students' work. Answers
will vary.

Page 107
Check students' work. 1. 6, 16;
2. 3, 13; 3. 4, 14; 4. 5, 15; 5. 2, 12

Page 108
Check students' work. 1. 2; 2. 5;
3. 1; 4. 4; 5. 7

Page 109
1. 17, 7, 17; 2. 19, 9, 19; 3. 15, 5,
15; 4. 13, 3, 13

Page 113
1. 1; 2. 10; 3. 10; 4. 9; 5. 6; 6. 10

Page 114
Check students' work.

Page 115
1. 16 = 10 + 6; 2. 13 = 10 + 3;
3. 15 = 10 + 5; 4. 18 = 10 + 8;
5. 11 = 10 + 1; 6. 14 = 10 + 4

Page 119
Answers will vary.

Page 120
1. heavy; 2. light; 3. light;
4. heavy; 5. short; 6. tall; 7. tall;
8. short

Page 121
Answers will vary.

Page 125
1. pencil; 2. envelope;
3. soccer ball; 4. backpack;
5. crayon; 6. spoon; 7. crayon;
8. straw

Page 126
1. 2, 1, 3; 1, 3, 2; 2. 1, 3, 2; 2, 1, 3

Page 127
Check students' work. Answers
will vary.

Page 131
Check students' work. 1 fish,
3 birds, 2 frogs

Page 132
Check students' work.
2 squares; 2 triangles;
2 circles; 3; 3

Page 133
3 squares; 6 triangles;
5 circles; 4 rectangles

Answer Key

Page 137
Check students' work. 3, 5, 4; red; blue

Page 138
6 people; 5 people; apple; grapes; 2 more people

Page 139
Check students' work. (3 squares, 5 circles, 8 rectangles, 5 triangles, 6 ovals) circle and triangle; rectangle; square; 3 more rectangle stickers

Page 143
Check students' work.

Page 144
Check students' work.

Page 145
1. 3, 6, 1, 5, 2, 4, 7; 2. 6, 10, 3, 12, 4, 1, 8, 11, 7, 5, 2, 9; 3. April; 4. 30; 5. Friday; 6. April 6th

Page 149
1. on; 2. in; 3. next to; 4. in front of; 5. under; 6. between

Page 150
Students should color the book that is on the floor, away from the table green. Answers will vary but should include the word *under* or *beneath*.

Page 151
Check students' work. right

Page 155
Check students' work.

Page 156
Check students' work.

Page 157
1. Check students' work.
2. Answers will vary.

Page 161
Check students' work.

Page 162
1. cone; 2. cylinder; 3. sphere; 4. cube; 5. pyramid; 6. cube; 7. cone; 8. sphere; 9. cube

Page 163
Check students' work. Answers will vary.

Page 167
Check students' work.

Page 168
Check students' work.

Page 169
1. square; 2. circle; 3. square, rectangle; 4. square, triangle; 5. triangle, rectangle; 6. circle

Page 173
square: 4 sides, 4 angles; triangle: 3 sides, 3 angles; rectangle: 4 sides, 4 angles; trapezoid: 4 sides, 4 angles; parallelogram: 4 sides, 4 angles; hexagon: 6 sides, 6 angles

Page 174
cube: 6 faces, 12 edges, 8 vertices; cylinder: 2 faces, 0 edges, 0 vertices; cone: 1 face, 0 edges, 1 vertex; sphere: 0 faces, 0 edges, 0 vertices; rectangular prism: 6 faces, 12 edges, 8 vertices; triangular prism: 5 faces, 9 edges, 6 vertices; square pyramid: 5 faces, 8 edges, 5 vertices

Page 175
1. triangle; 2. cube; 3. parallelogram; 4. cone; 5. square

Page 179
Answers will vary. Check students' work.

Page 180
Answers will vary. Check students' work.

Page 181
Answers will vary. Check students' work.